THE DYNAMICS OF TRIBAL DEVELOPMENT ISSUES AND CHALLENGES

THE DYNAMICS OF TRIBAL DEVELOPMENT

ISSUES AND CHALLENGES

Dr. Sachindra Narayan

GYAN PUBLISHING HOUSE
NEW DELHI-110002

The Dynamics of Tribal Development
Issues and Challenges
(*Anthropology, Tribals Studies*)
Rs. 490

ISBN : 81-212-0687-1

Published in 2002 in India by
Gyan Publishing House
5, Ansari Road, Darya Ganj,
New Delhi - 110002
Phones : 3282060, 3261060, Fax : (011) 3285914

E-mail: gyanbook@vsnl.com

Website: http://www.gyanbooks.com

Lassertypesetting at: A.A. Computer
Printed at : Mehra Offset Press

Contents

Preface

Anthropology : The science of MAN in its totality has to shoulder the great responsibility and face the challenges of the 21st century based on its experiences of the early centuries. Physical anthropology as well as social anthropology is in great demand at the global level because of success as well as failure of various developmental measures experimented in different parts of the world. A single developmental experiment has a different result in different countries. Why? This is becoming very important question for Anthropology. Realising the role of Anthropology World Bank, Asian Development Bank, etc. are having a good number of Anthropologists as their consultant. So much so that, UNESCO has declared 21st century as the century of Anthropology. There are many anthropological "realities", produced and reproduced in local and global systems of thought and knowledge. This awareness encourages us to clarify the issues we confront in the light of the insights. We have gained as anthropologists since the Torres Strait expedition of 1898. The role of Anthropology in understanding human societies and the problems they face in the 21st century needs to be discussed much by the export of the field in order to allow to grow anthropology in its own way.

The three decades experience of a practicing or action anthropologists suggest that the anthropologists needs to orient themselves with micro studies at the global level. The tools, techniques and research method needs to be suitably developed to serve the MAN of 21st century. Now no longer holistic method and the geneological method remained the method of anthropology only. In the age of multidisciplinary research method, these two are widely used in other social sciences also. The research methods and techniques of anthropology requires a little more chiseling for 21st century anthropology because in the next century most of the time on services will be required for quick appraisal, action oriented research programme, environmental degradation and genes, etc.

Anthropology has long tradition of field work which we are missing at the close of 20th century. What B. Malinowaski, Margret Mead, Raymond Firth, Robert Redfield, Ruth Bendict, Milton Singer and in India S.C. Roy, G.S. Ghure, L.P. Vidyarthi, S.C. Dubey and others did is a milestone in the subject and their work also presents model before the present generation and I hope the future generation will also take inspiration from these work. The scientific research technique of anthropological field work begin with the rapport building, interviewing the respondents with the help of a questionnaire or schedule or interview guide, life history, case study, geneological table, photography, etc. The oriental model of field work based anthropology has grown to super computer based model. In super computer model or statistical or mathematical or geometrical model adopted the close of this century is loosing the field touch and human brain based on ethnic-cultural value model which to me, is the fragrance of anthropology. Therefore, after having 30 years experience of field work I feel that the research methods suiting to our needs ought to be developed.

In this book, which is collection of my articles written and presented in different seminars and symposium during 1997—98, I have tried to present the facts at the micro level based on anthropological data collected during different phases of field work through anthropological research methods and techniques.

The first article is on custom and traditions of the tribal without which the life of the tribal will be colourless and lifeless. The custom and traditions of Garo, Chenchus and Oraon have been discussed in this article.

The second article is on W.G. Archer who has done very important work in the field of anthropology of law. Mr. Archer has codified the tribal customary law which has become a base for the demand of self rule by the tribals these days.

The third article highlights that the Indian Anthropology have remain devoid of studies on development of tribes on Gandhian approach of development. Though the country is known for Gandhi but Indian anthropology has failed in its responsibility by conducting studies on those tribes who changed their life under the impact of Gandhi and are still practicing Gandhian way of life.

The fourth articles is on the globalisation of primitive. The tribal economy known for economy of exchange based on cooperation and exchange is now being injected with the input of globalisation of economy.

The fifth article is on a socio-political movement which is now a century old movement but yet to achieve its objective. The article is on the Jharkhand

Movement from its origin to the functioning of Jharkhand Area Autonomous Council and of Jharkhand state.

The sixth article is on folk dance and folk songs of tribes of Bihar. This article again talks on the tradition of the tribes.

The seventh article is on the strategies for solving energy problems of tribal Bihar. Energy is the important input for development. The tribal Bihar is quite rich so far resource base of energy is concerned.

The eighth article is on rural development where I have talked of two models of development. Here by mentioning the experience of Rajasthan I have tried to emphasise the role of right of information. The crucial issue facing the rural poor today in India is very simple. Does a poor illiterate peasant, landless labourer, artisan and rural women have a right to demand from the government details of development expenditure carried out in their village.

Do they have right to ask for copies of bills and vouchers and names of persons who have been paid wages contained in mustor rolls on the construction of schools, dispensaries, small dams and community centres that on paper have been shown to have been completed. If they are willing to pay for these documents to be photo copied, which could also serve as certified copies in case any police cases have to be registered against village officials or politicians for embezelement, corruption or misappropriation, can the government refuse.

The last article of this volume is on rehabilitation process. The paper primarily focusses on anthropological, psychological issue which are natural outcomes of displacement resulting in rehabilitation because of development projects. It discusses anthropological-psychological consequences on the people affected by these projects and attempts to provide a basic frame work to understand its anthropological-psychological perspective.

I am thankful to the administration, library and typing streams of this Institute who always remained cooperative and helpful in completing my articles and books. I am equally thankful to my wife Shobha who always bears suffering with me along with our children Shiwani, Subhash and Savidhi. I am much thankful to the publisher for publishing this book.

Sachindra Narayan

January 2002

1

Jharkhand Movement to Jharkhand State: A Development Model

I

India has a rich cultural milieu. There are different types of people in India. Tribal India is a distinctive picture by itself. It must be remembered that India's tribal population estimated at 54 million is almost equal to the total population of the United Kingdom. India has the second largest population in the world, next to Africa. The tribes differ considerably from one another in race, language and culture, in their myths and customs and their longings and aspirations. They are the most colourful people of India and they represent a true synthesis of Indian culture. The tribes of Jharkhand present a spectacle of striking diversity, but it is the diversity marked by varied racial characteristics, variegated with cultural traits, plurality of occupations and diverse linguistic traditions that lend lustre to the cultural mosaic of the state. Different tribes live at widely different stages of development, there an tribes living in the remotest corner of the state in a primitive stage and in abject poverty. Each of these groups, no matter what their number, is a proud community participating in the national life yet retaining its own identity. They go to define the basic value of Indian civilization.

Jharkhand means a place full of forest and in reality Jharkhand is full of forest and minerals. Nature has made this region, the richest in the country in terms of national resourses but the MAN living in the region is the poorest in the country because of the OTHER MAN'S attitude.

Without going into the historical antecedents of the first settlers of this region, it is worth mentioning that they have been severely exploited since the days the DIKU entered this region. We have incidence of such exploitation during the 4th century A.D. Dikus mostly immigrated in this region during the Mughal era and made their way into the life and culture of the tribals. The 'head hunting ceremony' among the tribals is one such example of exploitation. Around the Sixth century A.D. the Mundas and Oraons jointly selected 'Manki (leader) who was not the sovereign of the land but had to play a prominent role during wars. A descendant of this Manki was later made a tributory of the Mughals by 1585. One Manki Durjansal was imprisoned by the Mughals for his return from the Gwalior jail in 1660 he surrounded himself with Hindu countries and merceanries who he made 'Jagridar's of Munda and Oraon villages with the right to collect and enjoy taxes from those villages. The immigrant Jagridars and Thikedars in course of time, introduced land rent in the Chotanagpur region and gradually ousted many of the original inhabitants of the land for their inability to pay rent or reluctance to render begar or forced labour to the new masters. Thus, the transfer of ancestral tribal lands to outsiders began as early as the 17th century reducing the tribal peasants to mere cultivators of landlords, who in turn paid a share to the Maharaja of Chotanagpur, who then paid a share to the Mughal emperor.

By the middle of the 18th century, the adivasi society began to lose its own distinctive qualities under the influence of a larger Hindu society. Its disintegration was expedited by the introduction of social division of labour in the form of the caste system. Pressure of immigrant Rajputs, Brahmins and other high caste Hindus and the exploitation by these newly emerging mahajans, *thikedars* and *jamindars* completely shattered the adivasi economy. In 1771, Jharkhand came under the jurisdiction of the East Indian Company. The company initially subordinated the Maharaja of Chotanagpur almost in the same way as did the Mughals. But as they were actually integrated in revenue from the land, they introduced a permanent legal and administrative structure to ensure regular and smooth collection of revenue. British administrators gradually introduced money economy, individual ownership of land and a police system to control tribal uprisings. The traditional right of the tribals over land and forests as well as the age old Panchayat systems thus slowly gave way to the forces of modernisation. The Permanent Settlement Act of Lord Cornwallis in 1793 legalised individual proprietorship in land and led to a further alienation of tribal lands. Indiscriminate destruction of forests and unplanned mining in the region pauperised the tribals. The tribal population, were gradually transformed into a vast army of coolie (labour).

Almost all the 'Rajas' of the Jharkhand region accepted British supremacy and started paying rent to the crown by the end of the 18th century. Thus, the whole administrative machinery of the former 'Raja' became a useful instrument in the hands of the alien rulers to exploit the indigenous people. By the beginning of the 19th century, Chotanagpur came under a frontier system of administration. The East India Company was at the top of the ladder, followed by the Maharaja of Chotanagpur, then a number of local Rajas, mostly of non-tribal origin and finally the Thikedars appointed by the Rajas to collect rent directly from the peasants.

II

The tribal people of India are a part and parcel of the India population. There is need to understand their problem. Most of the problems concerning the tribals stem from the fact that very few people in India know the problems that they face. In the past there occurred bloodshed and rebellions, specially among the Nagas and the Mizos.

It is indeed difficult to define the term 'movement' precisely, but for our present analysis, it may be defined as a deliberate, organised, conscious effort by members of a society to construc a more satisfying culture. I have adopted the term without its usual qualifying adjectives, social, revivalistic-political movements, so that it helps to include various diverse forms of group phenomena whose components can be identified in the analysis variations in the level of each of the component and in the mix of these in a social phenomena explain the various forms of movements.

The study of tribal movements has been a relatively recent development in the field of social anthropology. Ironically the growing volume of literature on the subject reveals the lead taken by historians, administrators and social workers in the documentation of these movements. Anthropologists have generally been preoccupied with the study of the elements of social organisation and their interrelationships. The understanding of wider process which have a profound bearing on the network of interrelationships has not been much in evidence. Since the mid sixties, however, a few of our social anthropologists have started becoming active in this field of study and have explored the impact of macro-histrocial and economic processes on small, enclosed and encysted systems. However, a critical evaluation of the date reveal the absence of adequate emperical evidences. The concepts used in the processing and interpreting material and the tools used for generating the material are borrowed from research situations elsewhere. As a result the Indianness of the Indian experience is not reflected particularly well. There is also a great deal of overlapping in the time dimensions. There are variations in the tribal movements from region to region. In the north-east the tribals are in an overwhelming majority, the tribal system, both social and economics, is relatively secure. Tribal movements in this area have been essentially political and secular in nature. The situation is far more complex in central India. The tribals have been reduced to a minority in many areas and have been exposed to the processes of rapid change.

Industrialisation has come about in a big way, the centres of industrial development have shifted from the coastal and metropolitan pockets to the tribal regions. Agrarian issues have also been in the forefront. Therefore, the tribal movements in this region have developed an essentially agrarian character, even while the tribes have emphasized ethnicity and articultural demands of a political nature (Narayan, 1988).

III

Intermittent tribal movements against the diku (exploiters) is a characteristic of the regional history of the 19th century. In 1768 the Paharias revolted against the British exploiters. In 1978-99, the Bhumiji and the Kurmis also revolted against the British. Singhray and Binarary Maniki revolted against Diku thikedars during 1831-32. The East India Company defended the rent collecting thikedars under attack even with troops. The Mundas, Hos. Bhunias and Oraons of Chotanagpur joined hands to fight against the double oppression of the Diku-British alliance. The 'Santal Hul' rebellion led by Siddhu and Kanhu in 1855 was a violent expression of the simmering discontent and tension among the Santals against the exploitation by the non-tribal mahajans, jamindars and British merchants. The Santals claimed the right to the lands which they used to cultivate. In many areas people were organised on the pattern of private armies, equipped with bows, arrows and battle axes. Several cases of arson, looting and even killing of mahajans were reported. Mopherson (1909) opines that apart from the oppression of the mahajans and landlords, a deeper sense of feeedom Santal yearning for independence, a dream of the ancient days when they had no overlords, perhaps a memory of prehistoric times when they were themselves masters of the Gangetic valley and had act been driven back by the Aryan invaders was instrumental in giving rise to the uprising. The movement though it had an apparent ethnic bias, was not confined to the Santals alone. Though the Santals provided the leadership even the artisan castes like Kumhars, Telis, Kamars, Gowalas as well as the Momins, all of whom had developed close relationship with the Santals through the ages were intimately connected with the movement against the tyranny of outsiders. The Khuwar movement, a Hinduised reform movement, also took place to encourage acculuration at a greater level. Another anti-Diku agitation took place during 1875-95 known as Sardar Larai (leaders' war) to establish the right of tribal peasants over land by driving away alien landlords. The Birsa Munda uprising of 1895-1900 was primarily directed against the British and the non-tribal landowners. It aimed at establishing a 'Birsaite Raj' with Birsa as its new king, after driving away all the foreigners not only the Britishers but even the Hindus and Muslims from the region. Birsa fought on economic, social, political and religious fronts. Land, forest people and religion were the key issues in this uprising. The Tana Bhagat Movement was organised under the leadership of Jatra Oraon around the year 1914 with a promise of millennial era of rule free from foreign scattlers on their land. It was an ethnic, revivalist movement among Oraons which called for purity of life. The leaders launched a 'no rent agitation' against the Diku land owners. Jatra Bhagats' followers came in contact with Mahatma Gandhi and joined the Non-cooperation movement.

IV

All these movements upto the 20th century basically centred around the issue of exploitation and deprivation of the indigenous people by the migrants and the ruling elite. In the beginning of this century, quite a number of institutions led by Christian missionaries and students emerged and introduced social reforms in the lines of tribals. Such movements aimed at checking the drinking habits among the tribals and rescuing them from the clutches of money lenders by forming co-operative societies. One such society, the Roman Catholic Cooperative Society was formed in 1906 and played a significant role in raising the standard of life of the Christian tribals in Chotanagpur. There were also societies for the promotion of education among the tribals which provided the nucleus for the later political movements. One such society, i.e., the 'Christian Association' was formed by the Lutheran graduates in 1898 and was renamed the 'Christian College Union' in 1918 after the Catholics joined it. The first students' belonging to various tribes of Bihar was established by Dr. Rajendra Prasad in Patna and a Christian students conference was convened at Hazaribage in the year 1910. The Christian tribal students were concerned about the socio-economic upliftment of the tribals. The first organisation for the said purpose was organised by the Lutheran Christians and J. Bartholmew, a student of St. Columba's College, Hazaribage, formed a society called 'Chotanagpur Unnati Samaj' in 1915. It aimed at the social, economic and political development of the tribes of Chotanagpur. It was basically an urban, elitist organisation with very little influence in the villages. The Simon Commission arrived in India in 1928. The members of the Chotanagpur Unnati Samaj, led by Bishop Van Heeck and Joel Lakra, took the opportunity to place a memorandum before the Commission seeking special privileges for the tribals and urging the Commission to consider the demand for a separate administrative unit in the Chotanagpur region. The effort did not succeed.

The desire to overcome the urban Christian orientation of the movement was evident in the formation of a Kisan Sabha in 1931 under the leadership of Theble Oraon, a non-Christian, who along with Lorentitus Burla, left the Unnati Samaj to organise the Sabha. The Kisan Sabha, however did not attain any significant success as its programmes were not effective in Chotanagpur and Santal Pargana.

In the Government of India Act 1935, Chotanagpur was described as a partially excluded area and was put under the special responsibility of the Governor under the special section 92 of the Act. The Chotanagpur Unnati Samaj opposed the provision through a number of resolutions and held quite a few meetings, without much success, as the government stood firm about the provision. However, when elections were held in January 1937 in accordance with the provisions of the new Act, all the candidates fielded by the Unnati Samaj and the Kisan Sabha were defeated, as Congress swept the polls. Electoral reverses of the tribal candidates in the 1937 elections led to a change in the attitude of the tribal leaders and an attempt was made to bridge the gap between the Christians and non-Christians among the tribals. The result was the constitution of Adivasi Mahasabha in 1938, a monolithic organisation into which the Unnati Samaj and Kisan Sabha were merged. Contrary to its name the Adivasi Mahasabha did allow the non-adivasis of the region to participate in its activities, at least officially. The Bengalis who considered themselves unsafe in Bihar and the Muslim League, planning to build a corridor linking the east and west wings of Pakistan, also provided moral and mater all support to the Mahasabha. The Mahasabha in 1939 and gave a call for the creation of a separate province for the tribals. Later during the Second World War when the Congress ministry in Bihar resigned on October 31, 1939. Jaipal Singh supported the British Government and its war efforts and helped them to recruit tribals for the British army. The Adivasi Mahasabha was not initially a political party and more or less remained outside the mainstream of nationalist politics. It sought representation in the Bihar Pradesh Congress Committee but did not get it. Subsequently it contested the 1946 General Election on its own and was routed by the

Congress at the polls. The defeat was largely because of the emergence of 'Adim Jati Seva Mandai' a social reform organisation, formed by Dr. Rajendra Prasad to conduct welfare activities among the tribals and 'Sanatan Adivasi Mahasabha' formed by Theble Oraon, as a counterpoise to the Adivasi Mahasabha. The link between Adivasi Mahasabha and the Muslim League was broken in 1947.

V

Justin Richard, a tribal leader organised the United Jharkhand Party late in 1948. The party was open to both the tribals and non-tribals. Jaipal Singh joined the new organisation after some initial besitation. On March 5, 1947 at a conference of the Adivasi Mahasabha held at Minidisala in Ranchi, the Jharkhand Party was formed with Jaipal Singh as its president and Idsen Daba as the secretary winding up the Adivasi Mahasabha Jaipal Singh did not hesitate to arouse promordial loyalties of the tribals and used violent means to put an end to north Bihar' dominance in the region. Ethnicity was gradually replaced by regionalism as the rallying point for the Jharkhand Party and the militant movement gave rise to an organised political party. This was partly because of the recognition of the tribals need for special protection under the Constitution of India and the provisions inserted under the Fifth and Sixth Schedules for their emancipation. The Jharkhand leaders were probably also influenced by the stand taken by the Congress Party that language, not ethnicity, should determine the formation of a province. Many elements of the Congress Socialist Party and quite a few members of the money lending community identified as Dikus joined the Jharkhand Party during this period. The area of Jharkhand was enlarged to include lands inhabited by the Chotanagpur tribals but falling under West Bengal, Orissa and Madhya Pradesh. Thus, a new phase of constitutional participation based on regional sentiments dawned.

In the first General Election of 1952, the Jharkhand Party fought the elections with the call for an 'Alag Prant' and became the largest opposition party in the Bihar Legislative Assembly by winning all the 32 seats from South Bihar and three Lok Sabha seats from Bihar alone, Jaipal Singh himself became in M.P. This electoral victory gave a new impetus to the party and the movement.

The State Reorganisation Commission was formed in 1953 with Fazle Ali as its Chairman. After the formation of the Commission, the Jharkhand Party submitted a memorandum signed by 34 MLAs, on April 22, 1954. It demanded formation of the State of Jharkhand within the Indian Union, comprising the districts of Chotanagpur, Santal Pargana and parts of Gaya, Shahabad, Bhagalpur and Munger districts of Bihar, four tehsils of Mirzapur district of U.P., Surguja district of Chhatisgarh and districts of Keonjhar and Mayurbhanj in Orissa. K.M. Pannikar and H.N. Kunzru, two members of the States Reorganisation Commission, visited the Chotanagpur region from January 27 to February 10, 1955 and had to face impressive demonstrations by the members of the Jharkhand Party. The Commission, however, in its report did not agree with the idea of a separate Jharkhand state due to lack of viability of the regions as a linguistic unit.

In the second General Elections of 1957 the Jharkhand Party strength was marginally reduced to 28 seats. Between 1955 and 1961, a number of anti-moneylender agrarian struggles led by Santal activists of the Jharkhand Party took place in Santal Pargana. Prominent among leaders was Satrughan Besra, an MLA from Jamtara.

However in the 1962 General Elections, the Legislative Assembly could find only 20 members of the Jharkhand Party. This happened largely because of the Christian vs non-Christian issue among the tribals. Jaipal Singh, facing severe criticism for his dictatorial attitude, also sought refuge under the Congress umbrella. Thus, the Jharkhand Party merged with the Congress in June 1963 surrendering the popular party symbol 'cock' and its legal identity.

VI

The merger dealt a severe blow to the movement and ushered in an era of confusion in the politics of Chotanagpur region. Jaipal Singh was included in the Bihar Cabinet led by Pandit Binodananda Jha, who saw this as an opportunity to penetrate into the tribal belt which had so far eluded the Congress influence. However in August 1963, Jha had to resign as Chief Minister, under the Kamaraj Plan and his successor K.B. Sahay relieved Jaipal of hispost of Education Minister and appointed S.K. Bage as a Minister. Not only Jaipal Singh was dislodged from his ministership in the Bihar Cabinet, but most of his followers, particularly the senior ones, turned against him. They declared the merger to be illegal and started reviving the old party. The party spirit though revived was fragmented and lapsed beck to its ethnic character.

During the fourth General Elections of 1967, an anti-Congress wave was evident in the Chotanagpur plateau. Tribal leaders in the Congress, with a Jharkhand background fared badly. Jaipal Singh scraped through with a very narrow margin, while S.K. Bage, a Minister in the Bihar Cabinet, forfeited his deposit. Those opposed to the merger fought as Independents and succeeded in winning eleven seats in total. After this election, Bihar passed through a period of political instability and there were experiments in coalition governments from 1967 to 1972 while the lack of any unified political group of the tribals further added to the confusion. In the midst of growth a number of splinter groups were formed and factionalism was at the top when kartik Oraon, a Hindu tribal appeared on the scene. In November 1968 Kartik Oraon appealed to the A.K. Chandra Committee visiting Ranchi to divert the money spent on Christian tribals to the welfare of the backward non-Christian tribals. Soon Kartik Oraon was rewarded with the Vice-Chairmanship of the Chotanagpur and Santal Parganas Development Authority, located at Ranchi. He also won the Parliamentary Election of 1967 and 1971. By this time the Bihar Scheduled Areas Regulation Act of 1969 put restrictions on the alienation of tribal land to non-tribals and provided for their restoration. This was an important legislation in preventing further loss of tribal land to the outsiders and in restoring the confidence of the original inhabitants.

On May 1968 David Munzani organised the 'All India Jharkhand Party' which was dominated by Christians and naturally could not resolve the Christian vs non-Christian rift. Begun Sumburi was named President and N.E. Horo the General Secretary of the party. The party was soon divided into Begun faction and Horo faction. In 1972 N.E. Horo formed a new party known as 'Jharkhand Party'. On March 12, 1973 he submitted a memorandum to Indira Gandhi, the then Prime Minister, for creation of a new State. This was a modified version of what Jaipal Singh submitted in 1954. In 1968 Justic Richard formed yet another party in Santal Parganas namely Hul Jharkhand which got seven seats in the 1969 mid-term poll of the Bihar Assembly.

Another radical group 'Birsa Seva Dal' was quite active during 1967-69 specially in the urban areas of Ranchi and Jamshedpur, founded by Lalit Kuzur and had Moses Guria as its General Secretary. The Dal organised violent attacks on non-tribal landlords and led mass demonstrations in the urban areas clamouring for a tribal state.

Almost during the same period a social reform organisation, namely Shivajee Samaj appeared in 1969 under the leadership of Shibu Soren to fight the evils of liquor, moneylendings, etc. Shivajee Samaj soon took the shapre of a movement and spreaded over a large area of 'Jharkhand' including parts of Puruliya district in West Bengal. The movement reached even remote villages, fought against the exploitation of landlords and started 'Dhan Kato Andolan' (forcible harvesting). 'GrainGolas' (village grainaries) were established to help the poor tribals at the time of crisis.

Such measures made the movement very popular among the tribals and mobilised a large section of the landless tribals around the Samaj.

VII

Shivajee Samaj was gradually transformed into 'Jharkhand Mukti Morcha' (JMM) with Binod Bihari Mahto as its President and Shibu Soren as its general secretary. The Marxist co-ordination committee of A.K. Roy also lent able support to the Morcha. Some of the Naxalite groups operating in the Dhanbad area also provided moral support to the movement. Thus, radicalism found a new expression under the banner of Jharkhand Mukti Morcha and the movement got transformed significantly on many counts. The Morcha projected itself as a radical party fighting against internal colonial exploitation of the tribals of Bihar. The Morcha not only demanded a separate State but also promised better living conditions for the tribals. The JMM decided to recover alienated lands from moneylenders and big peasants in North Chotanagpur, an area where the Jharkhand Party was not very strong. More than hundred cases of land riots and violent clashes between the tribals and the Mahajans were reported from the region. The agrarian radicalism of the JMM was combined with its interest in cultural revivalism. The ancient practice of 'tribal self government' was partially revived. The 'Baisi' (assembly) was revived in Santal Parganas, without pleaders or court fees, to deliver simple justice to the local people. Traditional collective farming on common lands was reintroduced in some areas.

The JMM also widened its base, at least in Dhanbad, by embracing the mining and industrial workers, most of whom came from the neighbouring States. Thus, an attempt was made to bring the workers and the peasants closer on a common platform. Thus, the JMM also took the non-tribals, peasants and workers in its fold. The JMM also projected for the first time the non-tribals as their leaders like Suraj Mandal, Binod Bihari Mahto and A.K. Roy. The protagonist of the Jharkhand state kept a low profile during the J.P. Movement in 1974, though Jaya Prakash Narayan himself was in favour of creating smaller States in India. The General Elections of 1977, held after the Emergency, ushered in the Janata rule both at the Centre and the State of Bihar and saw a virtual route of the regional forces in the Chotanagpur region.

During the Janata rule in Bihar, interestingly, all the political parties, including the Congress, created their own Jharkhand cell to appeal to the pro-Jharkhand sentiment of the tribals. The otherwise dead political movement started gaining ground again since 1978. Shibu Soren emerged as a true mass leader in Dhanbad and Santal Pargana. During 1978-80 he organised violent rallies and mass demonstrations against moneylenders, big landholders and mafia leaders. The 'Jungle Bachao Andolan' centering around the forest areas of Singhbhum also gained ground during this time. In January 1980, during the seventh General Election, Shibu Soren's charismatic personality helped his followers to win the Parliamentary and Assembly elections.

In the eighth Lok Sabha elections Shibu Soren lost along with his followers but in the subsequent Assembly elections the JMM won 14 seats. The combination of Shibu Soren and Suraj Mandal of JMM started a vociferous demand for a separate Jharkhand state. In 1985, 52 members of the Bihar Legislative Assembly, representing the Chotanagpur region sent a joint memorandum to the Prime Minister demanding central administration in the Chotanagpur region. Meanwhile the tribal students formed the All Jharkhand Students Union (AJSU) on June 22, 1986 taking a cue from the tribal student's movement of Assam. Suraj Singh Besra became its President. This further fragmented the movement.

In the 9th Lok Sabha Elections of November 1990, the JMM emerged as the strongest Jharkhand group in tribal, Bihar. It captured three Lok Sabha seats and 19 Assembly seats in Bihar. In the subsequent Lok Sabha elections of 1991 the JMM contested 6 seats in the Lok Sabha and won all of them in alliance with the National Front. But the rise in political power did not necessarily mean the solution of the problems of the poor tribals of the Jharkhand. The poor tribals were still there where they were in the 40s but their leaders had become progressive. The Jharkhand now is not only a favourite slogan of the tribal leaders but also of the non-tribal leaders. The Congress-I, BJP and Janata Dal—all national political parties are giving weight upto the problems of the Jharkhand Movement but any satisfactory solution of the problem is not within sight. In subsequent election JMM lost its representation in Parliament. However in Rajya Sabha only Shibu Soren managed to represent JMM. Later on one more seat went to JMM in Rajya Sabha with the help of Samta and BJP.

The Jharkhand Movement today is at a major cross-road in its history. The statement of the Union Home Minister S.B. Chavan on September 8, 1992 in Pune that the "formation of either a separate state or union territory of Jharkhand is the only solution to the Jharkhand problem" has breathed fresh life into a movement which had lately been gathering moss. The statement of S.B. Chavan has been largely welcomed by the tribal leaders and the elite of Jharkhand region.

The entry of the controversial former Union Minister of State for

Home Subodh Kant Sahay into the Jharkhand Mukti Morcha created a furore and significant confusion among the leadership as well as the rank and file of the party. With his entry the Jharkhand Mukti Morcha formally split into two factions, one led by the Charismatic Shibu Soren and the other by Krishna Muradi. However, the momentum lately gathered by the Movement seems to be largely unaffected, though what political fall out ensues from this development can hardly be determined at this juncture.

The firm stand taken against the division of the state by Laloo Prasad Yadav, Chief Minister of Bihar has, in effect united all factions of his Janata Party, as well as received the support of practically all the major political parties, who are against any further fragmentation of the State.

The Bhartiya Janata Party (BJP) is also demanding a separate state comprising the same geographical area but with a different name, i.e., VANANCHAL. CPI, IPF, Congress and other national and regional parties are also in favour of a separate state with their own nomenclature. With the change in the political scenario, we find that all political groups are favouring the creation of a separate state autonomous council. This sudden change in the attitude of the political parties is, perhaps, the realization of the slow pace of development.

On November 24, 1993 a five day South Asian Indigenous people's Conference was held at Tonto, Chaibasa, Bihar to discuss the problems of the indigenous people of South Asia. This conference came with a new demand of Kolhan state. A Journalist's report appeared on the first page of the Hindustan Times of November 25, 1993 (late city edition, published from Patna, Vol.8 No. 88) mentioning that "the final day of the five-day South Asian Indigenous people's Conference here today was marred by an ugly scene when the Deputy Commissioner of West Singhblum, Sajal Chakraborty, had to ask the co-organiser and head of the Nepal delegation, Pradhan Prajuli to get down from the stage following the latter's refusal to allow the Jharkhand Mukti Morcha (Maradi) MP Krishna Maradi to address the meeting.

Prajuli, a University Professor in the United States, allegedly threatened the Deputy Commissioner and told him not to allow the JMM leader on stage or else the D.C. would be taken to task by the tribals of the Kolhan region. Chakraborty, visibly distributed ever Prajuli's comments, ordered him to get out of the stage at once and detained him for sometime. Later, on the request of other delegates, he was released. Krishna Maradi pointed out that the demand for a Kolhan state is unjustified as it would mean recognition to a particular tribe and language". It is evident from this report that the purpose of discussing the problems of tribals got diffused in this Conference.

A similar conference was organised in September 1992 at Dumka to discuss the problems of the tribals which ultimately demanded the creation of a separate state for Paharias.

Such National/International Conferences have failed to discuss and identify the problems of the people of the region rather they worked as stimulant in diverting the attention of the Government/policy framers from concentrating on the development of the tribes.

Such conferences/discussions in last 47 years have not been able to bring all the tribes and their leaders on a common National Platform. At the national level we do not find any such platform where the tribals identify themselves as one unit. The polarisation of different castes may be 'high' or 'low' forward or backward has become an independent factor in Indian democracy as well as in forming policy at the national-level. But the tribals are yet to make such a dent in national polity. But I am sure, based on empirical date, that by 2020, the tribals are likely to emerge a stronger political force.

I have concluded in my book, Jharkhand movement: Origin and evolution (p. 18) that "All these manoeuvring and political powerplays have only helped to confound an already confusing scenario. The poor tribal living in a remote area of the Jharkhand region does not know where to turn. Adding to the confusion is a demand by the Paharias of Santal Pargana for a separate state for themselves".

JAAC : Composition and Powers

With the inauguration and constitution of the Jharkhand Area Autonomous Council (JAAC) on 9th August 1995, the movement for autonomy in this region seems to have turned a new leaf. For the first time in the history, the tribals have succeeded in getting an administration machinery which fulfills, albeit partially, their aspirations of self rule. The mercurial and firebroad leader of the JMM, Sibu Soren is the right choice for JAAC Chairmanship. It may be mentioned him that the tribals have been guaranteed that the chairman, who is also ex-officio Chief Executive Councillor (CEC) of JAAC will always be a tribal (Section 15 (i) and 21 (i)). However, there is no restriction on the office of the Vice-Chairman, who is ex-officio Deputy CEC (Section 16 & 21 (i)). He would normally be a non-tribal. During the inaugural term Suraj Mandal has been appointed as Vice-Chairman. The other 19 members of the Executive Committee would be nominated by the CEC in such a manner as to give adequate representation to ST, SC the OBCs and Women (Section 21 (ii)). Provision of a Council Secretariat headed by an officer of the rank of additional secretary to the

Government of India known as Chief Executive Officer, has also been made (Section 37 (i)). He will function as the Secretary of the General Council as well as the Executive Council (Section 37 (ii)). The Secretary and other employees of the Secretariate will be appointed by the Government of Bihar in consultation with the CEC and they will work under his small supervision, guidance and control (Section 32). The JAAC has been empowered to recommend legislation on subjects assigned to by the state legislature (Section 31 (i)). Besides, the General Council is entitled to make by laws and regulations in respect to subjects assigned to it:— 1. Public Health, 2. Hospital and Dispensaries, excluding medical education, nursing training and research institutions, 3. Tourism, 4. Vocational Education, 5. Agriculture, 6. Construction and maintenance of rural roads, 7. Cremation and Burnt Grounds, excluding those maintained by municipalities, 8. Hats, Market and Fairs, excluding those being managed by the Agricultural Marketing Association, Municipalities and District Boards, 9. Minor Irrigation, 10. PHED and Sanitation, 11. Dairy Development, 12. Fisheries, 13. Bee Keeping, 14. Sericulture, 15. Primary and Secondary Education, 16. Management of Buildings and Lands under possession of JA, 17. Rural Development, 18. Small cottage industries, 19. Minor wells, 20. Welfare departments—all programmes, 21. All programmes relating to urban development, 22. Repair, renovation and maintenance of medium and major irrigation projects, 23. Forests, excluding protected forests and also settlement of forests of any shape, 24. Use of canal water for irrigation purposes other than those canals which pertain to medium or major projects, 25. Recommendation for settlement of government land for agriculture and animal husbandry, 26. Management of cattle food, 27. Regional planning and implementation externally aided projects in the area with reference to subjects transferred, 28. Tribal subplan and welfare, 29. Cultural affairs including theatre and drama, 30. Sports, 31. Youth welfare, 32. Animal husbandry, 33. Visual statistics including registration of births and death, 34. Weight and measures, 35. Local Transport, 36. Food and civil supplies, 37. Tribal welfare, 38. P.W.D., 39. Municipal Corporation Improvement Trust, District Boards and other local self government and village administration, 40. Panchayats, 41. Recommendations to the State Government regarding electricity.

District Covered by JAAC

Godda

Sahibganj

Pakaur

Dumka
Deoghar
Dhanbad
Giridih
Hazaribagh
Kodarma
Palamu
Lohardaga
Gumla
Ranchi
Purbi Singhbhum
Chatra
Bokaro
Garhwa

Since the inception of JAAC it is under controversy, but I feel that JAAC is a great achievement of the age old Jharkhand movement. Now they can go one step more than that is the statehood demand. JAAC is one forward step towards getting a Jharkhand state. Only yesterday (25.5.97) it was in the news that the State Government through its secretary had a talk for giving more power to JAAC with its Chief Sibu Soren. Let us wait for the future strategy of Sibu Soren.

Production of Minerals

According to Indian Minerals Year Book 1970, the Jharkhand region of Bihar produces 27.77 per cent of total minerals of India compared to 0.47 per cent by the rest of Bihar.

Sl. No.	*Name of Mineral*	*All India value Rs. lakh*	*Total Production as % Total Mineral Production*	*Percent Jharkhand*	*Production Rest of Bihar*
1.	Copper	374.8	0.77	100	Nil
2.	Keanite	261.1	0.54	85.0	Nil
3.	Quartizite	16.0	0.03	60.5	5.3
4.	Mica (Crude)	202.4	0.41	58.5	Nil
5.	Asbestos	21.4	0.04	53.0	Nil
6.	Apatita	9.8	0.02	48.6	Nil
7.	Coal	29292.7	54.27	44.5	Nil
8.	Sand	10.4	0.02	37.3	Nil
9.	Fireclay	44.8	0.09	33.0	Nil

10.	China clay (Processed)	84.1	0.17	28.7	Nil
11.	Bauxite	174.6	0.36	32.4	Nil
12.	Iron Ore	3680.1	7.59	22.4	Nil
13.	Limestone	2302.3	4.75	3.7	7.5
14.	Manganese Ore	771.9	1.59	0.6	Nil
15.	Pyrite	56.3	0.12	Nil	100
16.	Other Minerals	12733.9	26.28	4.37	Nil
	Total	48447.6	100.00	27.77*	0.47

*Figures excludes value worth 1.15 per cent accountable by other mineral produced in Bihar for which the distribution between Jharkhand and the rest of Bihar is not readily available.

Imbalanced Development of Jharkhand Versus Rest of Bihar

	Major Items	*Tribal Bihar*	*Rest of Bihar*
1.	Contribution to revenue	70%	30%
2.	Expenditure of revenue in	20%	80%
3.	Irrigated land of the total	5%	50%
4.	Rural Electrification	5%	40%
5.	Paved Road per 1000 kms.	5 km.	20 km.

Jharkhand contributes seventy per cent of the total revenue of Bihar but only twenty per cent of the total expenditure is incurred in Bihar. The disparity in development between Jharkhand and rest of Bihar is glaring. Jharkhand produces almost the entire electricity of Bihar but rural electrification Jharkhand is meagre in comparison to rest of Bihar. Most of Jharkhand is not covered by railways and therefore it depends mainly on road. Dumka and Hazaribagh the commissionary headquarters are not connected by rail.

To Conclude this paper I feel that the movement like Jharkhand will never die primarily because it is people's movement. We have data from Thiblo Oraon to Sibu Soren, the leadership has changed, the political party has changed but the movement has not changed. Demand for a separate state is still there. The tempo of the movement go up and down but do not dwindle or die. After the formation of JAAC I presume this movement may reach to its logical end before we enter to 21st century because of formation of coalition government at centre in which all political party have their say. Also because the activists of different movements demanding for a separate state has formed a joined platform and if they make a pressure group it may succeed. Also because of the process of change occurring in our society the Scheduled Tribes are going to rule this country very shortly.

VIII

Jharkhand movement has resulted into a reality and on 15th of the November 2000, Jharkhand became a new state of India. The non tribal living in Jharkhand are comparatively more happy then the tribals because majority of the tribals are illiterate and therefore are unable to reap the benefits of a new state. No political party has come out with the programmes meant for the development of the tribals. The state is suffering from violence, infections disease, unemployment, inadequate agricultural production, non-availability of irrigation facility, drinking water etc.

W.G. Archer, a well known administrator of the region long back recommended for self rule. Infact the tribals have their own administrative and judiciary system which needs to be incorporated in such a way so that such institution become helping hand for governance.

The inter and intra tribal conflicts is going to be one of the foremost important problem for the law and order. It can be well contained by inducing innovative indigenous developmental inputs. The parallel system of governance already functional in the state can be curbed by creating employment opportunities and accelerating the small growth rate.

The mines and minerals are attracting NRI investors. It ought to be planned in such a manner so that it may lead to overall balanced growth of the state.

The state has been created in the name of tribe and their culture. Therefore both tribe and their culture needs to well knitted with the non tribal and their culture so that the policy of the Indian constitution is not diluted. The primitive and dwindling tribes one of nine types but they are dieing therefore special component programmes be designed accordingly. The Chief Minister, Chief Secretary of the Jharkhand must be clear about the model of development of the Jharkhand state. It is felt that the combination of Kerala-Andhra-Maharastra-Madhya Pradesh model will ideally suit for the development of Jharkhand state and after a decade no body will suffer from lopsided development in Jharkhand. The Felt Need based programmes and policies be drafted and implemented in the interest of the development of Jharkhand state. The Hindu model of development needs to be examined carefully before it is experimented. Though all political party claiming for Chief Ministership have exploited the Hindu sentiment without understanding its developmental model.

Probably this is the only tribal region where Mahatma Gandhi lived for a few days and influenced a section of tribe so deeply that they call themselves as Tana Bhagats. The developmental model of which Mahatma Gandhi made experiments there needs to be adopted with certain modifications. The Vision and strong will to translate the vision into reality at the apex level of polity and administration are the pre-conditions for the development of Jharkhand state.

The tribals are going to decide the future of Indian Polity like that of U.S.A. Presidential election of 2000. My writing of early 80's and late 90's have suggested that by 2020 Indian Polity will depend upon tribal polity. The tribals need to be united as Indian Tribals.

IX

The recommendation for the *development of* the Jharkhand state and of its people are:

Based on my last 33 years research experience of the region I feel that first of all people of Jharkhand be made aware of the constitutional provision made for them because majority of them are unaware of its even to day.

2. Identification of local natural resources in the light of development of the people and of the state and its best exploitation.

3. Linkage between local natural resources and state resource be established.

4. A realistic need based sustainable local-regional—state plan be prepared with the participation of people from each segments with a support team of expert.

5. The political-administrative will for the development of state needs to be properly streamlined and augmented.

References

1. Meherson, H. (1909). Final Report on the Survey and settlement operations in the District of Santal Parganas, Calcutta.
2. Narayan, S. (1972). Jharkhand movement: Origin and evolution, New Delhi: Inter India Publications.
3. Sharma, A.P. (1988). The Jharkhand Movement: A Critique, Social Change, 18 (2).
4. Narayan, S. (2000). Jharkhand and its development. Gyan Publications.
5. Naryan, S. (2000). Jharkhand Movement to Jharkhand State.

2

W.G. Archer and Self Rule: An Anthropologist View

W.G. Archer (1907—1979) carried his passion for poetry and interest in art into his administrative career in Bihar which spanned a period of sixteen years from 1931 to 1946. As an administrator, he was given assignments that ordinarily came one's way in those days. Archer used his postings in rural areas of Bihar to cultivate his interests in Indian art and literature and to develop new dimensions of interests in Indian ethnology and anthropology. His first posting in the rural district of Arrah (now Bhojpur) stimulated his interest in the cult of Birnath, the God worshipped by the Ahirs whose wooden image he saw while on a Christmas tiger shoot in Rohtas. The investigation continued until 1939 when he visited, accompanied by good aided, the entire belt lying across the Sone and Ganga rivers and the Chotanagpur and Shahabad forest regions. He studied the regional styles in wood of the Cattle God, Bir Kuar also known as Birnath. The story of this cult and of its hero in wood and stone is told the Vertical Man, A study in Primitive Indian Sculpture published eight years later in 1947. This cult has since gained in popularity.

A visit to Puri in 1932 put Archer in touch with the Puri Painters and a sub-divisional officer of Madhubani (1933-34) aroused his interest in the famous folk art of Mithila revealed within the houses struck down by the devastating earthquake of 1934. However, it was his many years of service in tribal Bihar that shaped his interest in tribal poetry. As Assistant Settlement Officer on training at Ormanjhi in Ranchi district, he had his first exposure to the tribes. Later as subdivisional officer of Gumla, predominantly inhabited by the Oraon tribe, he learnt the Oraon language as part of his official duties expansive days to collect Oraon poetry, marriage songs and riddles through process serves who during their visits to villages would collect and write down for him the words of the songs. These were published later in The Blue Grove (1940) and the Done and the Leopard (1948). Verrier Elwin described the first as a "work of the greatest significance and importance, which set a new standard in translation from Indian poetry and opened a new doorway in the anthropological investigation of the Indian tribes. While working as District Magistrate of Purnia district, Archer came in contact with the Santhal tribe for the first time. Back in Chotanagpur as Census Superintendent of Bihar (1939-41) at Hazaribagh, he travelled all over the province and collected a mass of anthropological, all of which could not be published owing to wartime economies, through a good deal of tribal poetry in the vernaculars collected with the aid or many tribal young man was published in tribal languages, Oraon (Lil Khora Khakhal), Ho (Ho Durang) and Kharia (Kharia Abug) during 1941 and 1942. The census report of 1941 turned out to be a controversial document, it was generally supposed that the estimate of the tribal population given in the 1941 census was exaggerated as compared to that of 1931 census and as revealed by the 1951 census data.

This phase with a brief interruption in Patna a collector reached a climax via four years stay in the Santhal Parganas first as Deputy Commissioner (1942-45) and then as Special Officer of the Judicial Department to record the Santhal laws (1945-46). Archer also become Joint Editor with Varrier Elwin of Man in India founded by S.C. Roy, of which many issues were devoted to specific administrative and literacy themes, the two together also gave it a poetic and aesthetic bias. Archer had close links with scholars and administrators who were active in the area of tribal studies and welfare, Sir W.V. Grigson, Chrisoph Von Furer Haimendorf, Philip Mills and Verrier Elwin who was in the process of formulating his approach to tribal problems in the 1940s. Again as part of his official duties he learnt Santhali. He continued to take interest in tribal poetry and organised the collection of Santhal poetry which was published in three volumes, Hor Soren, Deon Soren and Hor Kudum.

Those also provided the material for the Hill of the Flutes: Life Love and Poetry in Tribal India, a portrait of the Santhals (1974) published almost thirty years later. This book does not belong to the category of traditional monographs. It does not deal with the material traits or the mode of production; it does not describe the range and dimensions of culture contact, though the Santhal have been among the most acculturated tribes. It takes up only some aspects of Santhal life, life cycle, ceremonies and festivals, sex and love. Although there is little that is original about the material used to describe Santhal life and institutions, except the poetry, the account derives strength from the case histories adduced to support the traditional accounts of the Santhal customs and from Archer's personal experience. The narrative begins with a description of the ideal, happy setting, the village, the clan system and the world of spirits (Bangas); this is followed by a portrayal of the life cycle.

Archer's duties as Deputy Commissioner of Santhal Parganas (December 1942 to June 1945) brought him into close contact with the Santhal. He had to decide cases involving the Santhal and had thus the first hand opportunity to observe the points of conflict that arose out of the application to the Santhal of the statutory laws (the Indian Penal Code, Civil and Criminal Procedure Codes) and the Santhal's adherence to his customary laws. Many others before him had commented upon the disastrous impact of the imposition of the colonial laws and judicial system on tribes and watched with dismay the erosion of the tribal system. Attempts had been made to enclave many tribal areas and introduce the single line administrator in which the officers combined judicial and executive functions to provide quick relief for tribals and to consult the tribals before disposing of the cases involving them. But such experiments remained like island and elsewhere the tribals had been assimilated into the administratior and judicial system of the Raj. In the mid 1930s many administrators and anthropologists had commented upon the dichotomy of tribal and colonial legal system and pleaded for the recognition of tribal low. It was this recognisition of the autonomy of the tribal system and the laws which could best be administered in the interest of the tribals themselves that lay behind the codification of Santhal laws. It was expected that this would help the courts understand Santhal laws and dispose of the cases involving tribals in the light of their own customary laws. Such a measure was recommended in very general terms by the Santhal Pargana Inquiry Committee in its report (1937) which suggested framing of a self-contained Tennancy Act, updating of Santhal Parganas mannual, compilation of the rulings of courts, etc. The committee observed in its report:

There is a real danger that an attempt at complete codification may result in a rigidity and fixity of law which would remove the elasticity of the system which is so essential in dealing with a district that is gradually advancing from a state of backwardness. This must be avoided... The main outline of the rights of landlords, pradhans, raiyats, etc. should be incorporated... Generally, therefore, we do not wish to alter the law but to state it as clearly and as fully as possible.

The Committee spoke of the agrarian laws in particular while recommending codification of the laws in general. Archer described pointedly the genesis of the enquiry to codify the Santhal laws under his supervision as special officer as follows:

For many years prior to the appointment of the Santhal Parganas Inquiry Committee, the absence of a complete statement of Santhal law had been a notable defect in the district administration. It has always been assumed and rightly assumed that in all civil matters the Santhal had a tribal law of their own and that this should be applied by the courts in the decision of their civil suit. It has also been assumed that officers trying such suits would know what the law was. This latter assumption, however, was often believed by facts and there can be little doubt that in the absence of a full statement numberless wrong decisions were given in the past. The matter was further complicated by the fact that during the present century the law regarding the rights of women appeared to be changing officers holding Santhal courts were, therefore, frequently at a loss to know what principles to apply. It was with a view remedying this state of affairs that the Santhal Parganas Inquiry Committee recommended that a memorandum should be prepared stating the present position of the law and it was with a view to implementing that recommendation and rectifying a very serious weakness in the civil administration of the district that I was placed on special duty to prepare the present report (Archer papers).

The objective of Archer's Inquiry, therefore, was that "the Santhal courts should have a statement of Santhal law for without that it is quite impossible for them to do justice there was also a deeper and more remote reason for this:

Regulation III of 1872 had definitely provided for a record of Santhal law, the need for such a record has been conceded by McPherson in his settlement Report in 1909... none the-less all the settlements had neglected this point. I also pointed out that such a knowledge of Santhal law was very necessary for the settlements since without it a number of incorrect entries were made.

Archer also describes the mode of inquiry into the Santhal laws followed by him over the period from June 1945 to June 1946 in the last paragraph of his preface to civil laws. A band of young Santhali knowing officers, independent magistrate whom he mentions, helped him alongwith Santhal informants to collect, check and cross check the material on the laws at twenty centres in the Santhal Parganas to make sure that the account was as complete and authentic as possible.

All the principles recorded in the report were ascertained, checked and at least at 20 centres all over the Santhal portions of the district. These enquiries were made by 14 officers, 8 of whom were Hindus and 6 Santhals and they showed that there were how a clear and coherent body of Santhal law accepted and applied by Santhal throughout the district. To describe this law as "customary law" is completely to confuse the issue while to deny that a Santhal law exists is to ignore all the results of a long through investigation (Archer).

The evidence was fully checked all over the Santhal Pargana. The book was thus neither invented by an Englishman or a Diku (alien) but was an account accepted and attested by the Santhals.

As regards Archer's own competence to conduct and supervise an operation of this kind, he recalled his experiences as Munshiff and in various other capacities in Chotanagpur.

From 1934 to 1937 I was subdivisional officer at Gumla in Ranchi district and was ex-officio Munshiff. As Munshiff in Chotanagpur I certainly had considerable experience of civil justice in another tribal part of the Province... In addition to my service as subdivisional officer—Munshiff I have had six months experience of the Ranchi settlement in the Sadar Subdivision. I toured in Chotanagpur at my own expense for four months while on leave in India in 1938-39. I lived at Hazaribagh (from 1939-41) and toured widely through Chotanagpur (Archer paper).

The end product of the labour was three volume report on the Santhal laws which gave a complete and authentic picture of the state of the Santhal laws in the mid 1940s as they existed in the Santhal Pargana. The enquiry did not cover the non-Santhal (Diku) or deal with their perception of the law and extend beyond the administrative jurisdiction of the Santhal Pargana. As a definitive work on Santhal, it was beyond Kolean Haram's *Horkoren Mare Hapremkoreak Katha,* which was published in 1887 but written in 1872. It give a vivid account of many Santhal Institutions but in no sense a complete or systematic account.

Archer emphasised that his reports were not an account of the customary law but a statement of the present law as practised by the Santhal and not as Interpreted by the court.

It will be obvious from the many fact that Santhal law has changed in the last 50 years that the law cannot be called customary.

Archer submitted his reports in June 1946 and proceeded on four months leave. On return from leave he was posted as Additional Deputy Commissioner of Mok Ok Chung in Nagaland at the instance of Phillip Mills, Governor's adviser in Assam. Meanwhile, his reports had been examined by a Senior Colleague, Nilmani Senapati, a former Commissioner of Bhagalpur, who had also worked as Deputy Commissioner of Manbhum where a good number of Santhal lived and who was considered some sort of an expert on the Santhal. Senapati found the reports lacking in many particulars and containing criticisms of the officers and the official policies and he recommended that they should be filed. Archer who was at Dumka in December 1946 sent two letters marked "private and personal" to Binodanand Jha, Minister of the local Self Government Department which had commissioned the reports. These constituted Archer's spirited rejoinders to Senapati's criticism. Since these exchanges involve substantive issues, the distributor of a personal native apart, it will be necessary to present a summary of these.

Senapati contested Archer's thesis that there was a Santhal customary law because there were too many variations to suit the local circumstances that it was impossible to conclude that any custom existed Archer while rebutting this argument pointed out that there were a number of equally valid ways of dealing with situations which pointed to commonly accepted principles by the Santhals. These, he insisted represented a very clear body of tribal law. Knowledge of the principles and a statement of law were required for all, otherwise the civil court may do great injustice. Secondly Senapati thought that the Santhal would resent the impression created by certain statements in the first report that lived in a state of loose morals and that any Santhal could have the sexual act with any Santhal girl, married or unmarried, provided they were outside the restricted relationship Archers pointed out in reply that the moral code of the Santhal was governed by certain rigid tribal conventions and remedies were prescribed which in no way justified the inference that crimes were being continually committed. Archer also denied the change that the appointment of a woman as Manjhu would lead to chaos.

Senapati's criticisms of Archer's thesis in the third volume were more stricter as were Archer's rebuttals. Senapati appeared to have taken a serious view of an Englishman's and that too of a civil servant's criticism of the judicial system of Chotanagpur, of his references to the officers and judges ignorance of the tribal languages and tribal customs, etc. Archer explained that much the same criticism had been levelled by the anthropologist, S.C. Roy against the British system and that it was not the officers but the system that was to be blamed. If the British Government had done nothing there was no reasons why a popular Government should not take up the matter. Senapati also found Archer rather too critical of the handling of the Santhal and Santhal suits by regular Judge courts and of the High Court's ruling brushing aside the appeal to Santhal law, which Archer thought was wrong. However, Archer was on strong grounds when he tried to refute Senapati's argument that the settlement operation records only the existing right and does not create a right. The settlement operation in the Santhal Pargana is unique that the settlement officer and his officers function as civil court and unlike their counterparts elsewhere can thus decide points of title and create title. The jurisdiction of the civil court is specifically banned and the entries in the settlement records are the conclusive proof of right and custom and have the force of a decree. The Santhal Pargana Regulation of 1872 which provides for these were shaped by the historical experience of preserving the Santhal identity.

There could be other factors behind the burying of these reports Partition of the country was in offing. The Adivasi Mahasabha was becoming militant, in close league with the Muslim League, even though it had lost at the polls. Archer's view points could be misunderstood and provide grist to the political mill. However as one looks back at the debate, there will be little disagreement today in the light of our experiences of the regular courts functioning in tribal areas that there should be better understanding of the tribal customary laws in deciding cases of a civil nature involving tribals and that the codification of the tribal laws intrinsic to tribal welfare. Thus, there was a great deal in Archer's suggestion that the regular courts of law should show a better appreciation of the tribal custom in deciding cases involving the tribals. This is possible only if the tribal laws are codified. Unfortunately there has been little progress in the codification of tribal law in our country.

Codification of tribal laws together with the provision for legal aid should go a long way in meeting the tribal's grievances against the working of the present day legal system. A format of a larger survey in the field of Legal Anthropology is still to be worked out because while studies of tribal laws is much wider and covers the entire gamut of tribal life. Archer's work in this regard is an important contribution to the anthropology of law which is emerging as a major subdiscipline of anthropology. Hoebal says (Hoebel B. Adomson, The Law of Primitive Man: A Study in comparative legal dynamics, Athennum, New York, 1916) Modern Anthropology has its special contribution to make to the understanding of law for two reasons. The first is that the anthropologist, who has traditionally concentrated his studies. On small societies with single cultures, has been in a position to comprehend such societies, each in its entirety and so to deal with cultures as integrated working wholes. This has made possible the development of Comprehensive theories of cultural dynamics embracing legal phenomenon as but one aspect of culture. The second arose from the fact that anthropology is first and foremost a comparative science. It draws its data from all orders of society, primitive and civilised, prehistoric and contemporary and from all portions of the globe. It makes it possible to move such closer to the realisation of a genuine and empirical science of law. Such an approach to law through anthropology is one of functional realism by means of comparative legal dynamics.

It is relevant to our need not only to explore the many dimensions of law and society but also to evolve a system which should make understanding of the relation of law and society and of tribal law easier to administration of justice to the tribal quicker, lesser expensive and more affection.

To the value of tribal law to aboriginal society the anthropologists have given eliquent testimony. The tendency of the dead Varrier Elwin has said devotion to the soil, the power to stage a magnificant festival, the discipline of tribal law are things which modern village religion should not willingly let die. In the spirit of economic fellowship and the tradition of communal living, some primitive villages are a hundred years ahead of the modern world.

The recent enactment of Panchayati Raj act has given a new impetus to self rule which Gandhi use to say Gram Swaraj but the tribals had there is known by different terms among different tribes. The tribal women have been stripped off their traditional right of right to property. The tribals under different socio-political banners are demonstrating throughout the country for the revival of their traditional judiciary-administrative system, the impact of such demonstrations are yet to make any dent on the current administrative system of the Government. It is presumed that in case the traditional tribal administrative-judiciary system is revitalised and reorganised may minimise the pressures on existing, administrative-judiciary system. This may result into better administrative-judiciary system in 21st century, in case it is experiment specially when we are having Gorkhaland Council, Jarkhand Area Autonomous Council, etc. It deserves special attention and consideration of the Government at the Central as well as State level.

3

Anthropology of Customs and Traditions

Anthropology has come a long way from the early days of descriptive enthnography. The varied directions in which the present pursuit in search of specialised dimensions in anthropology have given rise to more than twenty specialisations. (Redfield 1966: 2, Bock 1974: 435). The scope and possibility is enormous and mind boggling. Many non-anthropologists have their own notions of what anthropology is about. Methodologically anthropology follows scientific method with a streak of humanistic empathy. The scientific approach in social sciences takes on varied hues depending upon the particular phenomenon accepted for investigation by the respective discipline. Thus, the method of investigation differs from our social science to another. Anthropology has developed its own unique and highly coveted style of investigation. Anthropology's method adopts a holistic perspective with an empirical approach for the data collection, primarily through the techniques like the participant observation and prolonged field-work in the language of the subjects of study as far as possible. Anthropologists are empirical to the core, in the sense that most of the data are collected by first hand field work; what is called secondary data is really secondary to us. No other social science immerses in the social reality as much as or as long as anthropology does for quite valid reasons. Thus, anthropology's effort is to build theories based primarily on the 'authentic', first hand data other social science disciplines like economics, political science, sociology and history do not rely primarily on first hand data. They find secondary sources of data quite enough for their purpose. By way of contrast, the anthropological research may be called micro studies as opposed to the macro-studies of other social sciences. But with extension of anthropological interest into the new areas of problems, certain tool and techniques of other disciplines are found useful by the contemporary practitioners of anthropology. Similarly the in-depth and authentic micro-level studies of anthropologists can add a tremendous amount of insight to the macro studies of others. Thus, today we find quite a bit of cross fertilization in terms of method in grappling with the emerging social reality but this inter-borrowing should not lead to the loss of the identity or methodological specificity of respective disciplines.

By and large anthropological research in India has focused primarily on micro-level studies such as tribes, peasant villages and social institutions such as caste, kinship, religion, economy and social control. Of course, there are important exceptions in the form of efforts to understand in the Indian society or civilization as a whole by anthropologists.

The anthropologist was a kind of cultural broker, who mediated between people through the knowledge and understanding which he generated. He made cultural contact easy. He helped control conflict, eliminate misunderstanding and reduce suffering. He helped to bring about culture change. He was a facilitator.

Johannes Fabian, a Dutch anthropologist, has recently drawn our attention to what he calls 'allochronism' i.e., the denial of *co-evalness* in time to the oppressed peoples with their oppressors. Here the role of anthropologist is debatable. After all, what have anthropologists generally worked for an independent India is a big question specially when we are celebrating the 50th year of the independence of India. Has it been for the success of planned development. Planned development is what has been designed for the people, not by them. Planned development resultant is widening the gap between rich and poor in the society. Poor has become poorest. The total population below poverty line is swelling day by day and we are simply playing with statistical jargons. Anthropologists need to come out with real plan for real development which is possible only through peoples participation meaning there by action research programmes. We ought to think for a new model of anthropological input for development of people only then we may survive otherwise we will perish.

Most Indian Social anthropologists have conducted their field studies within India or among emigre Indian in other parts of the world. In this respect they differ from Western anthropologist who studied primitive groups and much later peasants, in developing countries, frequently former colonies of Western powers. This difference has important consequences.

Modern academic discourse in the social sciences and humanities abounds in references to 'the other', and when Western anthropologists use the expression it usually refers to a non-white population, whom Westerners had regarded—and may still do as inferior, ignorant and needing their protection and guidance. The classical impirialist saw himself as the representation of a ruling race which had brought law and order and justice, and modern knowledge and technology to ignorant and superstitious natives. He carried on his shoulders the whiteman's burden of civilising the non-white world.

Anthropological knowledge, has from the very beginning been perceived as a means for achieving social purposes, for solving problems. If for Christian missionaries it made conversion easy, for administration it made governance so. Altogether it made the whiteman's burden a little bit lighter. Or, if you prefer, it enhanced his capacity to oppress the colonial 'others somewhat more strongly. Anthropological knowledge could be said in those days to have had its practical uses in making the exotic 'Others' appearless savage, more human, so that they could be acculturated, civilized, modernised, absorbed or just left alone. We should explore the ways and means by which our ethical beliefs themselves are enriched by anthropological knowledge. The gap between ethics and anthropology should be bridged. This calls for critical self-awareness.

Custom

A group behaviour pattern that may be established by tradition, by contemporary social habits, or religious percepts, as differentiated from a legally enforced institution (q.v.) customs are enforced by social disapproval of their violation. They lack the coercive backing of the sate (q.v.) and the sanctions of the mores (q.v.). Fashion and convention are less important than custom.

Man is a social animal whose genius flowers in his attempts to adapt himself to his environment. Like a silkworm spinning its own cocoon of silk man weaves around himself a delicate and intricate fabric of relationships that go to make up a composite culture.

The culture of people is embodied in the practices and observations of their day to day life, in their interactions with other people inside and outside their group, in their response to the forces of nature both within and without; in their understanding of the world around them seen and unseen.

In its broadest definition, culture refers to that part of the total reputory of human action as well as its products, which is socially as opposed to genetically transmitted. To quote E.B. Tylor "culture or civilization is that complex whole which includes knowledge, belief, art, morals, law, custom and any other capabilities and habits acquired by man as a member of society.

Customs evolve in a society in response to the needs of group living to put it simply, custom is unwritten law. It is not an arbitrary creation, however, but a collection product which is backed by social sanction and not infrequently becomes embodied in law or acquires the force of law.

In early societies and in strongly cohesive though isolated communities the force of custom has been persistent and well defined providing a unifying rallying point that offers an identity to each group while defining its relationships with other groups.

Particular customs take rest in each community and become a part of its way of life. Handed down from generation to generation through oral traditions they serve as a base for the development of a more refined concept of culture.

Tradition

A social situation process in which elements of the cultural heritage are transmitted from generation to generation by contracts of continuity; or the non-material cultural context so transmitted, having the prestige sanction of antiquity. By extension, in an institution where personnel terms over more frequently than once a generation, practices, ideas and lore transmitted over a series of such "turnovers" are called traditions.

The subjective aspect of the culture of a group which is transmitted from generation to generation through language in the form of meanings, values, beliefs, sentiments, attitudes and other ways of thinking, feeling and acting in so far as they are capable of verbal symbolization.

Garo

Garo is a matrilineal tribe of Meghalaya and had been divided into two ideally exogamous moieties (CHATCHI) viz. Sangma and Marak, each of which is again subdivided into many strictly exogamous clans (MACHONG). Of later origin are Momin, Shira and Areng as independent phratries that consist of the people of Gabil, Cheran, Hrinda and Dalbot and Nongbak machongs respectively of the Sangma moiety. It was also found that like those under Shira and Areng, the machongs affiliated to the Momin Chatchi were also alternatively affiliated to the Sangma Chatchi consequently all these three Chatchis, Momin. Shira and Areng are now considered as forming a 'sub-class constellations' of the Sangma Chatchi.

Chatchi is indicative of a larger exogamous group of the Garos descending from one of the founding Garo mothers and machong attributes an immediacy of matri-relations to the membership of relatively separate group centering round a common mother born of the earliest. In course of time Garos strict adherence to the rules of Chatchi exogamy lost its efficacy. The Chatchiries Slac Kened gradually and it gave rise to smaller exogamous divisions. This tendency for fission is operative in all the Chatchi groups.

In Garo Society, marriage establishes a perpetuating relation and a customary contract between the respective machongs (clans) of the principal male and female of a household as the husband of the inheritress daughter is to be ideally chosen from any of the sons of her father's machong, who becomes the only resident son-in-law of the household. He then takes the place of his father-in-law after the latters' death and thus the process in repeated. Other non-inheriting daughters of the household marry males of any machong other than their own and establish separate households away from the parents'. Each of these households then becomes the point of contact between the two machongs, one of the wife and the other of her husband. and this reciprocal contact repeats, itself with every occasion of marriage of the respective household's nokna. Machongs thus act as marriage regulating matrilineal descent groups.

Garo settlements over the district were divided into popularly known areas called Akhings, each under the ownership and control of a machong and is held in custody by on Akhing chief *Nokama* as the husband of the inheritress-female of the founder household of the Akhing. The nokrom of that house becomes the nokura on the death of his father-in-law, and his selection as a nokrom from among the nokura's nephew is generally a function of the mutual responsibility of the two machongs involved in the initial establishment of the household. A machang is too big a body to carry out all of its functions for the maintenance and protection of the nokma household as well as those of other members, male or female, who might have spread over different distant areas. Its responsibilities are, therefore, carried out by a smaller group of closely related kins within the machang called Mahari. In broad sense it is understood to mean the entire blood relations belonging to a machong and is also sometimes designated by the same name yet not of all of its members are to take special care of other members.

The concept of Maharis has two fold expressions as a consanguinous unit in relation to a member of a household (Kar: 1970). Man is as a consanguinous unit refers to a smaller body of the closer matri-relations, male and female of member in which the male matri-relations predominate with the maternal uncle being held in the highest esteem. Garos loosely refer to the latter group as Chrapante or Chratang rang, i.e., the elder and younger brothers, maternal uncles and the great maternal uncles. Consanguinous Mahari of a principal male or female of a household, thus, refers to their respective Matri-relations.

On the other hand, a functional Mahari refers to a small effective group of the above consanguinals and an affinal, i.e., the principal male and or his nokron in the household. These two males hail from the same machong and get domiciled in the same household identifying its interests and obligations with those of that household and participate in the decision making process of the consanguinous Mahari in respect of that household's affairs. The extent to which they can contribute to the decisions depends on their ability and success in controlling and effecting prosperity of the household.

The husbands of the non-inheriting daughters (Chawari) of the younger and elder sisters (Boningtany, Gumitang) and of the aunts (Aoang, Pajongtong) of the principal female of a household, sometimes join the deliberations of a Mahari meeting (Mahari Mela) in respect of that household. These husbands may contribute to the deliberations but the decisions are taken by the consanguinous unit of the Mahari and the household head and the nokrom always join that unit in arriving at those decisions.

For all practical purposes, the consanguinous unit is relation to the principal female of the household and its male head nokrom from the composite character of the functional Mahari. In this is found the representation of two machangs, that of principal female and of the principal male. This functional unit of the Mahari relates primarily to a household and is to consider all problems, rights and obligations of the household in the society, and has to act as a bridge between the principal male's and his wife's machangs. The focal point of power and formation in both the concepts of Mahari, however, has always been the chra, i.e., the male matri-relations of the principal female of the household. They can displace a female from the inheritance line of the household, and dislodge a nokma or a nokrom for his privileged position.

For such an overriding power of the chra, one should not underestimate the rule of the household head and his nokrom in the functional Mahari. In case of nokma households, it was found that during the pre-British days nokmas used to lead the forays in inter-akhing females or the raids against the plains people. In respect of properties of other general households, the male heads and nokroms are found to predominate in their acquisition and maintenances. In fact, the ability, fact and intelligence of a male head could help him in maintaining his indispensable position in the functional Mahari in respect of his household.

Functional Mahari as an institution was born out of mutual responsibility of two machongs in continuing a household.

Functional Mahari as an institution was born out of mutual responsibility of two machongs in continuing a household. It has assumed a bridge and buffer role between the concerned machongs of a household in uniting their interests and absorbing their shocks in respect of that household. This role has another dimension in the traditional custom of 'replacement'. It is the custom of providing for a second or subsequent husband/wife to the widow/widower from among the members of the deceased's machong. This custom has been developed to maintain the household as a continuing point of contact between two lineages which it had always contacted. The mutual rights and duties which accompany marriage and which bind together two lineages are known to the Garos as a 'Kim. Functional Mahari is the unit through which this inter-relationship or a kim could be sustained and risks of stability absorbed.

The principle of onsanga led to the rise of two institutions peculiar to the traditional Society. When the household need dies leaving behind his widow, nokua or in krom, his widow retains the rights, responsibilities and privileges of the principal female of the household and assumes the position of the Principal female of the house-old and assumes the position of the Principal wife of the nokran. Several authors considered this custom of getting married to the widowed mother-in-law with its consummation as the extraordinary feature of Garo Society. A close scrutiny discloses sporadic occurances of such a custom and the socio-economic relations usual to married couple are also found maintained by them. But consummation is neither enforceable by law nor rejectable according to Garo custom, but acceptable only to an extent that the logic of rules does not go beyond psychological possibilities. Another feature not yet discussed but no less remarkable than the aforesaid custom, has been what may be termed as stepdaughter marriage among the Garo. If the household head died leaving behind his widow and unmarried daughters, his Mahari would provide for replacement and the replacing member would accept the old widow as his Principal wife and her inheritress daughter as a co-wife. On the death of her mother, she assumes the role of the Principal wife.

Likewise on the death, divorce or desertion of a wife on acceptable grounds, the woman's Mahari would provide the husband with another wife from among her nearest kins. If sterility or disease occasions an absence of female child in the household, adoption from the principal female's nearest possible blood kins fills in the void to ensure continuity of the household. The principles of on souga and deragata are thus motivated to provide security not only to the old widow or widower but also to the person filling up the missing link and allow the household to adopt itself again to the continuous socio-economic relations in the society undisturbed by occasional gaps. They also provide for continuity of inheritance line in the same linkage. Functions and composition of a functional Mahari have thus a direct bearing on all these features of a traditional society.

The residence pattern in a Garo village provides a panorama of inter-Mahari relationship. Any marriage excepting that of anokna creates a new household in the village as the agetes are to start their own with husbands hailing from different Maharies and/or villages. Sons of a household may settle in the mother's village even after their marriage bringing in wives from a different Mahari or village. Though most of the sons of the household leave their nation village for staying with respective wive's household elsewhere, a few of them would always settle in their own village. Garos do not differentiate between the own children and the adopted ones. Hence an adopted male or female may start a new household after marriage in the same village.

Supernatural World

The Garos have a supernatural world of their own, that consists of those mites and memangs. Memang does not possess supernatural power but may excite fears in the mind of man. A Garo believes in the rebirth of the spirit or its temporary transformation into animal form. In mortuary ceremony they arrange for the return of the spirit of the dead into mothers' household. Mite are numerous and ubiquitous and when displeased become malevolent causing disease, death and damage to house and properties. Mite that are beneficient an equally ubiquitous embodying natural forces and when invoked into action.

Chenchus

During the Paleolithic age, the vast forests and park-lands of South India were interbited by bonds of nomadic people, who lived by hunting and the gathering of wild fruits, tubers and edible roots. The only traces left by these early food gatherers are crude stone implements found on the surface of many parts of the Deccan, so far no skeletal remains of the early races have come to light. Yet, in some isolated parts of the subcontinent, small groups of aboriginals persisted until modern times in a way of life which outwardly had changed very little since the Stone Age.

The Chenchus of Andhra Pradesh are one of these ethnic splinter groups, which were left behind by the material advance of the great majority of the South Indian population. Their present habitat is confined to the rocky hills and forested plateau of the Nallamalai Range, extending on both sides of the Krishna river. Until 1947 this river formed the border between the princely state of Hyderabad and the Madras Presidency of British India. At that time Chenchu were found both in Hyderabad and in British territories, but today their entire habitat lies within the state of Andhra Pradesh which contains the overwhelming majority of the speakers of the Dravidian tongue of Telugu, the language spoken also by the Chenchus. In their physical make-up the Chenchus confirm largely to a racial type described by anthropologist as veddoid, a term derived from the *Veddas,* a primitive tribe of Sri Lanka (Ceylon) like the *Veddas,* the Chenchus are of short and slender stature with very dark skin, wavy or curly hair, broad faces, flat-noses and a trace of prognathism. Though nolagir dressing in leaves like their ancestors, of whom the seventeenth century Muslim chronicler Ferishta gave a poignant description, they normally wear but the scantiest dress. The man small aprons suspended from a fibre or leather belt, the end drawn in between the legs, and the women cotton bodies and a length of sari cloth wound round their hips. There is no people in India poorer in material possessions than the jungle Chenchus, bows and arrows, a knife, an axe, a digging stick, some and baskets and a few tattered rags constitute many a Chenchus entire belongings. He usually owns a thatched hut in one of the small settlements where he lives during the monsoon rains and in the cold weather. But in the hot season communities split up and individual family groups camp in the open, under over hanging rocks on temporary leaf-shelters.

The basic unit of Chenchu society is the unclear family, consisting of a man, his wife, and their children. For all practical purposes husband and wife are partners with equal rights and this equality of status means that the family may live with either the husband's or the wife's tribal group. Each such group holds hereditary rights to a tract of land, and within its boundaries its members are free to hunt and collect edible roots and tubers. These used to be Chenchus' staple food, though we shall see that in recent years there has been a change in their diet and ways of subsistence.

The Chenchus are characterised by a strong sense of independence and personal freedoms. None of them feels bound to any particular locality and the ability to more from one group to the other allows men and women to choose the companions with whom they wish to share their daily lives. Marriage rules are based on the exogamy of patrilineal clans. As long as they observe the rules of clan exogamy young people are free to marry whomsoever they wish. Spouses can separate without any formality, but the abduction of a woman still living with her husband is disapproved of as immoral.

In the sphere of religion the Chenchus evince certain characteristic traits which distinguish them from the surrounding Hindu peasantry. Though they worship some of the deities prominent in the cult of Telugu villagers, they accord much greater importance to a powerful goddess, who has control over the game and the fruits of the forest. They also reserve a sky God who share some features, including name, with the Hindu supreme divinity Bhagavan and, though not believed to intervene very much in human affairs, is credited with power over life and death. The Chenchus' ideas of man's fate after death are vague and it would seen that various notions adopted from their Hindu neighbours have not been incorporated into a consistent body of eschatalogical beliefs. There is no definite idea that a person's fate in the hereafter depends on his deeds in this life, even though some Chenchus stories contain reference to incarnation. More widespread is the belief that a person's life-force (JIV) is derived from the supreme God and returns to him after death. The whole concept of a life force, a belief common to various Indian populations very likely stems from casual contacts with Hindus, and thus represents a comparatively new element in Chenchu thinking.

Oraon

The system of belief and practice, doctrine and behaviour which generations of Oraon society have gradually evolved and organised to face the unknown supernatural world and restore confidence to the mind of the community and the individual when it is shaken by crises and dangers constitute largely the customs and Traditions of Oraon.

The Oraon recognises a supreme deity symbolised by the Sun, superior and inferior nature-spirits and potentially beneficent ancestor spirits and maleficent spirits of certain dead human beings, besides beneficent and maleficent impersonal powers and forces. Tofemism has almost lost its religious aspect among the Oraons and Shwamism is involved in the Oraon's Magic rather than his Religion proper. And the Oraon's present religion may be described as a system of animism or rather spiritism set on a background of a still more primitive and vague animatism, in which the soul or spirit is not discriminated from the body or object it inhabits and an impersonal magic force of the nature of 'Mana' is attributed not merely to certain living beings and certain objects of external nature but also to some objects of human art.

Generally speaking, the Oraon ideas and doctrine concerning chiefly what he now regards as the more important personal powers and beings of the supernatural world and his ways of dealing with them or rather entering into relations with them constitute his Religion proper and his ideas about and methods of dealing with or rather dodging, controlling or pressing into service the innumerable supernatural impersonal forces and images that confront him at almost every step constitute his Magic. In fact, this Magic is rather pseudo-science than Religion.

In religion proper, the attitude of Oraon society, as that of other primitive societies, towards the supernatural is one of reverental fear in the presence of certain mysterious supernatural powers and beings and dependence on and conciliation and propitiation of land prayerful submission to them, and the result expected is averting the ill will and securing the good will of the supernatural beings and good luck to war in crops and cattle, health and progeny. Although it appears that originally name of the Oraon spirits was regarded as beneficent, contact with higher culture has since helped in investing a few of them with a beneficent on rather potentially beneficent nature.

The concept of personality that to some extent distinguishes the beings which are the objects of Oraon religions ritual from the forces dealt with by Oraon magic, is, however, often fluid and vague. No images of the deities and spirits are made. But the more important deities and spirits are sometimes visualised by individual Oraons in the shape of human beings or animals. Thus, the principal village deity Chala Pachcho or Sarna Burhia invariably appears in the shape of an old woman with matted locks of snow white hair. Some of the spirits, however, such as Chandi, the goddess of hunting and war, are remarkable for shape shifting which is indeed a characteristic of most of the spirits and deities of the Oraon pantheon. Except Ehala Pachcho and Devi Mai to whom both personality as well as a more or less definite form and individuality are ascribed, the other spirits though endowed with personality, are in fact group spirits of which there are more than one belonging to the same class and bearing the same or similar attributes and characteristics.

In Magic, the attitude of the Oraon is mainly one of defiance of and control and domination over impersonal mysterious powers and the result intended is the expulsion of evil or compulsion of natural or supernatural forces and powers in the production of desired favourable conditions or results such as good weather or rain.

Oraon religion, like similar other religions is primarily concerned with ancestral and certain other disembodied souls and Nature spirits and deities. The rites employed to establish harmonious relations with them are mainly supplications and prayers, offerings and sacrifice and the ceremonial sharing of sacrificial food beside certain special observances and taboos. Oraon Magic is primarily concerned with mysterious impersonal forces and powers residing mostly in natural or artificial objects and the instruments employed is dealing with them are principally charms and spells, adjurations and incontations as also certain traditional observances and taboos. The help beneficent personal spirits or rather of the supreme spirit is also sought to control these impersonal spirits or rather of the supreme spirit is also sought to control these impersonal powers or forces. Where as Oraon magical rites are all performed only as means to definite practical ends. Oraon religious rites, though mainly concerned with the immediate practical interests of life, are really ends in themselves and hallow and consecrate every thing they touch— food, sex, life and death— and stimulate emotion beyond mere response to practical needs.

The Oraon does not, however, attribute all the phenomena of Nature and all the good and ills of life to spiritual agencies to personal spirits, ghost and deities or to mysterious impersonal forces and powers. He recognizes that natural causes and conditions as well as human effort and human industry may ordinarily produce definite desired results. As the result of generations of observation of the processes of nature and through elementary reasoning based on such observation, this tribe, like other tribes on a similar level of culture, has accumulated a store of working knowledge concerning the effects of certain elementary mechanical processes, the apparent movements and functions of the some of the heavenly bodies, the habits and haunts of animals and birds, the properties of plants, fruits and flowers, barks and roots, the nature and qualities of different kinds of soil and the variations of the weather. This modest love constitutes the Oraon's rudimentary science. And the Oraon generally counts upon the regular and uniform action of such natural laws or sequences as tribal observation for countless generations has succeeded in ascertaining.

The Oraon's Magic begins where his positive science ends or rather his magic supplements and forms part of his science. And Religion Supplements and subordinates, but does not actually supplant his magic where as his science satisfies his intelectual need and his magic his practical needs, his religion is meant primarily to satisfy a psychic need.

Although the Oraon is cognisant of the natural causes of growth and is fully alive to the value of work and industry, he does not wait to seek the aid of religion and magic till his individual or tribal exertions fail and known natural laws appear to miscarry. By way of precaution he has come to employ magical and religious rites in conjunction with his normal activities of hunting, fishing and agriculture, in order that the course of such activities may run smooth and the desired goal may be duly attained without a hitch. He recognizes and appreciates both the natural and the supernatural forces and agencies shaping human destiny and seeks to utilize them both for his benefit according to his lights.

Although magic is not often found in combination with the Oraon's religion, the two never fuse, and the ministers of Oraon religion are generally different from those of Oraon magic, whereas religion among Oraon is essentially the business of the community, magic is ordinarily the business of the specialist.

Religion and Morals

The Oraon's standard of morality or in other words, of what is good and what is bad in human conduct, is determined by custom and tradition. The elders of each Oraon village community and Parha federation are the recognised custodians of such tribal custom and tradition. That standard though mainly subconscious in Origin, is known to have been materially influenced from time to time by individual Oraon elders of exceptional intelligence and force of character and much less frequently in the past but more other at the present day by younger Oraons of intelligence and character and zeal for social or religious reforms who have come in close contact with a higher culture, either Hindu or Christian or both.

The ideal of an Oraon's life at present is to live on good terms with his tribe fellows and with the gods and spirits and to possess sufficient lands and crops and cattle and a large progeny of healthy male children to be free from debts and to have enough to eat and drink so that he may be carefree and full of life and spend his leisure in drinking and jollity dancing and singing. The customary tribal code of morality requires the Oraon to avoid quarrelling with or harming other tribe fellows or seducing their wives and to pay one's debts. The traditional tribal code has come to recognise a divine sanction for moral conduct. Dharms, the supreme spirit, who sees all that men do, and as some say, knows all that men think is believed to be the guardian of morality, punishing all offences against customary morality with sickness, death or other calamity. Besides reparation to the wronged tribe-fellow, tribal custom prescribes the sacrifice of a white cock or a white goal to Dharms for expiation of certain offences against social laws. As for witchcraft and other forms of maleficent magic, the social sanction for such anti-social practices is at present expulsion from the community; but not long ago, the offender had sometimes to pay for such an offence with his or her life. Even if a person who has entered into a secret compact with some spirit to secure prosperity to himself and cause harm to other people and their cattle, escapes detortion and punishment at the hands of man and prospers in life for a time, it is an article of faith with Oraon that such an anti-social wrongdoer is sure to come to an evil end through the agency of the very same spirit; for such a spirit is proverbially prove to take offence at the slightest suspicion of remissness or neglect on part of its votary.

4

The Globalization of Primitive Economy

Social science data can be visualised as a matria with rows representing particular societies and columns standing for such entities as 'economy' and 'religion'. Anthropology has involved mainly the comparison of all cells in a column, i.e., cross-cultural studies of single institutions or of all cells in a row, i.e., studies of functional relationships between institutions of a single society. The major issue in economic anthropology is to what extent different formal calculuses of rationality or of "economizing" can be isolated in non eastern conditions. Economic anthropology studies how to induce continued expansion and secular change. Anthropologist study the breakdown of caste barriers in plural societies as changing patterns of income distribution and wage differentials between export and internal sectors. We are more concerned with how entrepreneurial behaviour relates to the context of economic choice for primitive farmers and shifting cultivators. As an anthropologist may another interest in the study of decision making at the levels of individuals business forms and nations and outside the classical context of supply-price demand balancing. Another close related and expanding economic field is business administration. For the anthropologist this field is perhaps most accessible through the work on growth of business organisation in primitive region. This enables us to see 'Organisation and managerial skills' as factors of production to be measured and considered in general analysis.

One of the most significant characteristics of the contemporary world is that the economic prospects of nations, regions and even individual communities are fundamentally inter-related. Investment decisions made by foreign firms, the currency devaluated of a distant government or the consequences of drought in another continent can all affect the livelihood of men and women thousands of kilometres away. In this sense at least, the concept of global economic system is not hard to grasp.

For as long as people have traded goods between different regions, which takes us well back into prehistory, societies have experienced some degree of economic interdependence and of the vulnerability to external events which entails. But for centuries, the majority of the world's population was engaged in meeting its subsistenceness within in localized, essentially self-sufficient societies. The evolution of an economy based upon the production and trade of marketed commodities was gradual. It began to emerge in Europe in the 16th century and reached fully global proportions by the early 20th century. The speed and intensity of change within in global economic system have greatly increased since the early 1970s. As a result it is more important to them even to understand since the early the dynamics of economic inter-dependence and their impact in different parts of the world.

The capitalist World-Economy is in turbulent era at the close of the 20th century. The post-1945 hegemony of the USA has gradually dissolved and no single state looks capable of taking its place. Military power may still be overwhelmingly concentrated in the USA in manufacturing production and financial leadership are more obviously associated with Japan or West Germany. Moreover, core periphery relationship at a globalscale are much less clearly defined than they were in 1960s when the distinction between the First World and the Third World was coined. The emergence of high income oil-exporting nations, such as Taiwan, not to mention the increasing size and diversity of the Chinese, Indian, Brazilian and Mexican economics make the global economy a much more complex and dynamic system, core states which feel vulnerable to the shifts in economic power as the USA and many European nations have in recent years are more prone to adopt protectionist trade policies, restrictly imports, than to favour global trade. Third World nations dependent upon international trade to finance their development an invariably the first casualties of such measures.

Recent and fundamentally novel developments have been summarized in terms of these developments.

1. The primary products economy has come 'uncoupled' from the industrial economy.
2. In the industrial economy itself production was come 'uncoupled' from employment.
3. Capital movements rather than trade have become the driving force of the world economy.

The relationship between individuals and social structure and institutions is a reflexine one we are shaped by our cultural environment but have the capacity, in turn, to shape it. The evolution of the capitalist World economy attests to the power and durability of its underlying cultural appeal. But at the same time society is in turmoil because the only legitimacy it has is social justice. The most hopeful future for the global economic system requires actions that attend to the twin goals of efficiency and equity. A similarly untidy combination of attention to global and to national priorities will be necessary. In an inter-dependent world, localized misconceptions can be costly.

The main thrust of the ongoing economic reforms consists of liberalisation, privatisation and globalisation. These terms refers to the different aspects of market economy to which the reform measures wedded. The reform policy and measures have gradually taking away the economy from the arena of a planned, mixed and socialistic economy which characterised the Indian economy during last four decades at a *Laissez Faire* economy. Globalisations at opening the economy to the foreign money, goods, technology and companies, since 1991 steps, legal and administrative, have been taken for facilitating free inflow and outflow of goods and capital. The process is going for last six years. The Economic scenario has undergone structural and directional changes.

Globalisation is considered as an important element in the reform package. But what constitutes globalisation? The term liberalisation has four parameters: (i) Reduction of trade barriers so as to permit free flow of goods across national frontiers; (ii) Creation of an environment in which free flow of capital can take place among nation-states; (iii) Creation of an environment permitting free flow of technology, and (iv) Last, but not the least, from the point of view of the developing countries, creation of an environment in which free movement of labour can take place among different countries of the world.

The advocates of globalisation were specially from developed countries, limit the definition of globalisation to only three components viz., unhindered trade flows, capital flows and technology flows. They insist on the developing countries to accept their definition of globalisation and conduct the debate on globalisation within the parameters set by them. However, several economists in the developing world believe that this definition is incomplete, and in case the globaliser's ultimate aim is to look upon the world as a 'global' village, then the fourth component, unlimited movement of labour cannot be left out. But the entire issue whether debated at the World Trade Organisation (WTO) or at other firms blacks out the 'labour flows' as an essential component of globalisation.

Globalisation which is more romantic world indicating the desire to integrate nation-state within the overall framework of the WTO is nothing but a modern version of the 'Theory of Comparative Costs Advantage' which was propagated by the classical economists to provide the theoretical foundations of unrestricted flow of goods from Great Britain to other, less developed countries at that time of colonies. It was argued that international specialisation benefits both the countries enter into trade relations.

The same argument has been brought forth by the advocates of globalisation now. They want an export led pattern of Government to replace the import substitution trade policies followed earlier. The imperialists nations during the 18th, 19th and 20th centuries also emphasised 'capital and technology flows' into the colonial countries. But they could force their will at that time because they were the rulers. Historical evidence reveals that all these trade, capital and technology flows helped the imperialist nations to drain out resources from the poor colonial nations. Thus, the imperialist nations at the cost of the colonial countries who remained in stagnation and poverty.

But the globalisers want us to believe that they are sincere now and as a result of the policies of globalisation, the developing countries would be able to improve their competitive strength and usher in a period of rapid growth. The developing countries are through various kinds of soft and hard pressures. As a result the process of dismantling trade barriers started and every years, since 1991, the Finance Ministers have been a money reduction of import duties.

Export of Selected Countries of the World

	Export Us $ billion		*As per centage of World export*		*Per centage increase in 1994 and 1995*
	1990	1994	1990	1994	1990
India	17, 967	25,000	0.56	0.58	39.1
China	62,091	121,047	1.95	2.80	95.0
South Korea	64,897	96,000	2.03	2.22	48.1
Mexico	26,714	61,964	0.83	1.43	131.9
World Exports	3,187,965	4,326,096	100.0	100.0	35.7

It is argued that this shall enable free flow of goods, capital and technology and the globalisation becomes a motivating force for nations to develop themselves on a faster pace that creates more gainful environment in the world scenario for each economy. For developing country like India, it opens access to new markets and new technology.

Ironically, globalisation is helping 15 per cent of the population of the industrially advanced countries. They are able to take advantage of unequal bargaining power at the WTO and force the developing countries (India being no exception) to open their potentially huge markets to foreign goods and services and capital and financial flows, without giving adequate concessions in return. Human Development Report (1996) categorically states "while globalisation has often helped growth in strong countries, it has by-passed the weak. The poorest countries, with 20 per cent of the world's, people, have seen their share of the world trade fall between 1960 and 1990 from 4 per cent to less than 1 per cent, and they receive a meagre 0.2 of the World's Commercial lending." The question, therefore, is Globalisation for whom?

Liberalisation in India has mainly come in as a result of disenchantment with the results of rigid control policy that the nation had drifted into. Since the middle of seventies when the economic situation improved somewhat, decontrol and liberalisation have been gaining ground with occasional reversals. The process has not been smooth but it has gone ahead. Shortage of foreign exchange, fiscal deficits and the need to prevent closures have acted as major brakes, but the desire for removal of regional disparities and group and individual inequalities have also been prevention forces. There has not yet been vigorous faith in the working of markets and has liberalisation led to spectacular successes. Hence their have been inevitable hesitations and some withdrawals. But unless the economic score suddenly changes for the worse, the onward march of liberalisation will continue. The speed will depend on how convincing the advocates of liberalisation can make their case and how the problems of poverty and inequality are affected by liberalisation.

Barter system prevalent among the tribes of India is a well recognised economic activity among tribes based on their custom and traditions. It is quite popular and functional. It has a social sanction and a fear of being visited by supernatural power upon those who violate the commandment. There is no high court to enforce the law of barter system but even then it is quite popular at the threshold of 21st century. The exchange made and rate very from region to region and also among tribe to tribe.

At the threshold of 21st century we are orienting the policy for the globalisation of economy and at the same time we found the existence of inter-economy in real situation. Barter economy is a hard fact and we anthropologist plans and policy makers are much concerned for this kind of economy specially when we are celebrating the 50th year of Independence, wishing to bring the tribals to the national mainstream. Thus, with this background it become necessary to know the impact of Globalisation of economy vis a vis primitive economy rather impact of new economic policy on tribals and also the response of the tribals towards new economic policy.

5

Folk Dance and Folk Songs of Tribes of Bihar

Generally speaking by the term tribe we mean a group of people living at a particular place from the time immemorial.

Anthropologically, the tribe is a system of social organisation which includes several local groups—villages, bands, districts or lineages and normally includes a common territory, a common language and a common culture. The elements constituting the tribe may or may not be coordinated by formal or centralised political power, ideally the term tribe implies large element of solidarity based on strongly shared primary sentiments. Such solidarity becomes contractual in nature as the tribal organisation becomes more formally organised. The point at which these latter characteristics become pronounced is, perhaps, a convenient place to distinguish between the tribe and the nation. In general anthropologists agree on the criteria by which a tribe may be described: common territory, a tradition of descent, common language, common culture, a common name, political system, simple economy, religion and belief, primitive law and own educational system.

Constitutionally, a tribe is he who has been mentioned in the Scheduled List of the Indian Constitution under Article 342 (i) and 342 (ii).

According to 1991 census there are thirty tribes in Bihar; they are:—

(1) Asur (2) Baiga (3) Banjara (4) Bathudi (5) Bedia (6) Bhumij (7) Binjhia (8) Birhor (9) Birjia (10) Chero (11) Chik Baraik (12) Gond (13) Gorait (14) Ho (15) Karmali (16) Kharia (17) Kharwar (18) Khond (19) Kisan (20) Kora (21) Korwa (22) Lohara (23) Mahli (24) Mal Paharia

(25) Munda (26) Oraon (27) Parhaiya (28) Santhal (29) Sauria Paharia and (30) Savar.

Among them Mal Paharia, Santhal, Sauria Paharia and Savar are exclusively found in the district of Dumka, Deoghar, Godda and Sahebganj. The rest of the tribes are found in the plateau of Chotanagpur. The Bhumij and Kora are found in both the places, i.e. in Chotanagpur plateau and in the old Santhal Pargana division. Economically, the Munda are the dominant tribes of Bihar and numerically Santhal and Oraon are dominant tribes of Bihar. Some of the tribes like Tharus, Kheturis, etc. have not been included in the list of the scheduled tribes, though they are tribes.

According to some census the total tribal population of Bihar is 5,810,867 in which 2,915,492 are males and 2,895,375 are females. The tribal population of Bihar is 8.31 per cent of the total population. Among them 93.77 per cent are found in rural tribal Bihar and remaining 6.23 per cent are found in the urban tribal Bihar. 16.89 per cent of the total tribal population of Bihar are literate. Among the tribes of Bihar we find ten dialects. Another interesting feature is that only 46.92 per cent of the total tribal population of Bihar are the workers (Main + Marginal workers).

The main occupation of the tribes of Bihar is agriculture. They practice two kinds of agriculture, i.e. settled and shifting. Majority of the tribes practices settled cultivation with their primitive agricultural technology. Tribes like Sauria Paharia and Korwa practice shifting cultivation which is known as 'Jhum' or 'Korwa' kheti (agriculture) in tribal Bihar.

The tribes of Bihar are rich in their culture, folk tales, folk songs and folk stories. They had an institution known as *Dhumkuria and Pelerpa* (Youth dormitory) where the tribal children and youth were imparted training in their culture. The objective of the youth dormitory was to train the tribals to become sincere, productive and useful member of their community. Children just after infancy were admitted in such dormitories. They were trained in folk dances. Even today, in their Akhra, they are trained how to beat the drums, to sing song and to dance. Each tribe has their own speciality in their dance. The movements of ankle, thigh and waist differ from tribe to tribe and dance to dance. The natural costumes, dresses and make-up also vary from tribe to tribe depending upon their ecology, environment and closeness from the forest. The tribes more exposed to urbanisation and industrialisation has imbibed 'notations' and 'Thirkanas (movement of the body) from the 'alien culture'. The dances and songs presented by the tribes of Bihar during Independence day and Republic day are not the Original tribal dances of Bihar rather such dances and songs are prepared under the impact of various agencies of cultural change. Trees, plants and such other natural objects have deep association with the songs and dances of the tribals of Bihar tribal songs and dances are also associated with their festivals, ceremonies and rituals. Each tribal village have *Akhra* where the male and the female of the village assemble to sing and dance together. Dance and song are not only the source of entertainment in tribal Bihar but are also associated with their religion, economy and above all with their culture. Such song and dance mould their lifestyle, world view and ethos. Song and dance are also being used these days for political purposes. 'Jani-sikar' (head hunting ceremony) is one of the folk dance wherein the dance and song depicts a historical fact of the tribal Bihar. Traditionally 'Jani-sikar' is observed once in every twelve years by the Oraon Women to celebrate their victory on the Muslims ruler of that time. It starts from the most important festival 'Sarhul' and continue for a month. During Jani-sikar women use to dress in men's fashion and moves from one village to another in groups to kill fouls, goats, hens, etc. and in the evening those things are distributed among the participants equally and finally the day's session ends with a feast and dance at village 'Akhara' (dancing ground).

One of the simplest definitions of Dance is that "it is an externalisation of emotional energy by means of muscular movement. It is practiced not only by man, and woman in every degree of civilization and culture, but also by many types of animals especially birds. It has age old variations bearing on time and clime and the culture of a people; sometimes it varies with religious fervour and sometimes serves as a mental stimulant. It has a definite note and form, rhythm and accent and with the inclusion of aesthetic elements, has become an art, not only attractive but also worthy of study. Dance movements are the result of an innate impulse for the release of surplus energy in the case of the young whether of human or animal origin. It is not surprising that the human being learnt the art of dancing from animals, specially birds, whose spontaneous and spirited exuberance of joy and delight form the common feature of bird life, the peacock, the most graceful and attractive of birds combines his artistic talents with the sexual appeal and takes the prime place as a dancer. Dances performed by the peacock are well known in the India as symbolic of both grace and rhythm and form only a sample of the numerous types of dances performed by the other birds.

Dancing has played an important role in tribal societies and the moderns have to learn much from the early dancers. There are social and religious dances and also the group dances and individual dances and also dances for couples of both sexes. Rhythmic beating and chanting which accompany the dances have been passed on to us from times past and have contributed much to the unification of social groups. Dancing in war also, has contributed to the entertainment and also to the group solidarity required for joint military action.

Folk dances of tribes of Bihar are many but among the most popular and known to the outside world is *Chchana*. There are some dances which are performed only by a particular tribe like *Dibloi* dance of Sauria Paharia. It is the only dance which is performed by Sauria Paharia during forest cutting for shifting cultivation.

The dances performed by the tribals while performing marriage rituals also vary from one tribe to another tribe but then there is some common marriage dances also. The Korwa, Bathudi and Binjhia dance performed while Kohbar ritual are going on is very interesting. Similarly dances performed during marriage ritual among Santhals of Bihar are different from the Santhals of Assam. Such differences may be because of ethnicity, ecology, environment, training in youth dormitory or so.

These dances need to be studied scientifically. At the moment we do not have any systematic scientific anthropological study on the dances of the tribes of Bihar. If you watch these dances closely, you will find that the folk dances are the mother of modern dances.

The folk songs of tribes of Bihar are very much known to the outside world. The *Jhumar* songs of Munda has become popular and we get cassette of these songs in the market, also. The folk songs of tribes of Bihar are again meant for various occasions. By listening a folk song you may decipher easily as to what ritual is being performed. Each ritual have a folk song of their own. Each tribe has their own folk song. The tribes who are economically at the hunting and food gathering level have a different kind of folk songs than those who are at the settled agriculturist level. We find similarity in the folk songs of Oraon and Munda to a greater extent but then they have folk songs which are sung only either by Oraon or Munda.

The folk songs and folk dances are greatly influenced by the advent of Televisions and Cinema in their villages. Now the tribals are watching different programmes in their home on their Television set which is causing great harm to the folk songs and folk dances. The educated tribal youth no longer take interest in their folk dance and folk songs and their children who are attending public school consider these songs and dances as derogatory to their current status. The gradual absence of youth dormitory in tribal Bihar is another contributing factor towards decline in tribal folk songs and folk dances.

The dress of folk dances are very colourful and vary from one ritual to another. The modern young generation of India are crazy in dancing. In cosmopolitan city one can find youth with pencil heeled girls do twirls and twists; a couple gyrates rhythnically, almost making love on the dance floor; a lone guy closes his eyes and lets go by himself.

Dancing is a form of expression. A creative way of unwinding, letting the guies flow and energise the self. As regards modern dance psychiatrist Dr. Achal Bhagat says Dancing is a sensation seeking activity for most young people. Like fast car and parties dancing make them an addict. Another angle is given by Freudian concept where most young people centre their life around pleasure seeking activities.

What I want to mention here that whether it is movement pattern, dress design or pleasure of the dances, all these have been derived from the tribal folk dances because they still preserve the ancient form of excellence of dance and so is the case with the folk songs. These are yet unresearched to a greater extent. I think in order to preserve the Indian culture we must have a systematic, scientific, anthropological record of folk dances of tribes. Some of the most known dances of India are well projected and well known but than the lesser known dances also used to be projected and highlighted in order to bring them to the national mainstream. We must not feel satisfied in our duty only by presenting one or two most known folk dances in Independence day programmes or in some similar occasions. Most of the time the participants of dances of such occasions are not tribals rather they are professionals which dampens the spirit of the folk artists. I am not advocating for ban of those programmes but I am trying to highlight is that such programmes be programmed in such a manner that it involves only folk dancers.

Our first Prime Minister Pandit Jawahar Lal Nehru was found of tribal folk dance and song. He had initiated many policies and programmes for the development and preservation of tribal culture. I presume the ethos of the policy of our first Prime Minister in this regard need to be cared to day also.

6

Rehabilitation Process of Tribal Villages in Bihar

The present paper is an illustration, how an anthropologist or behavioural scientist who are quite often turned as Social Doctor looks at the problems of "Displacement and Rehabilitation. The paper primarily focuses on anthropological, psychological issue which are natural outcomes of displacement resulting in rehabilitation because of development projects. It discusses Anthropo-psychological consequences on the people affected by these projects and attempts to provide a basic framework to understand its Anthropo-psychological perspective. It presents basic guidelines, action strategies for effective implementation of project with a view to minimise adverse anthropo-psychological effects on displaced population. It is also presumed that this paper would assist those who are the key actors in planning and implementation of these projects.

The paper is divided into three sections, in addition to conclusions at the end. Section A introduced the problem and presents the current scenario on the status of 'Displacement'. It is not intended to critically appraise the effects of all those who manage displacement and rehabilitation under development projects. However, a reference to the existing situation is made to provide a necessary feel to all concerned, to undertake planning and implementation of these projects seriously and search for realistic action strategies related to anthro-psychological issues leading to poor mental health (Jahoda, 1958). An attempt has also been made, to present Psycho-sociological Perspective of rehabilitation which can provide the basic framework for understanding and operationalising the issues associated with displacement. Section-B attempts to present description of psycho-sociological problems as perceived and felt by the affected population. Section-C focuses upon 'Strategies' for minimising psycho-sociological consequences of displacement and rehabilitation.

SECTION—A

1.1 Current Status of Displacement and Development

Development is an ongoing process which leads to commissioning of various kinds of development projects such as: Construction of new Irrigation Dams, establishing new Factories; Mines; Road construction; Railways and many others, which leads to Regional/National economic development. This often necessitates the government to acquire land which leads to 'involuntary displacement' of people from the original home land.

Development leading to displacement of people from their own land is inevitable. All activities mentioned above, force the otherwise stable, sedentary population to move away from the original places of home and work. It uproots people from their original land and creates psycho-sociological stress leading to many dysfunctional consequences. More often, both social and economic benefits of such developmental projects are not shared equally by displaced population.

The problem of displacement is normally related to economic aspects but truly speaking, it has more of psycho-sociological implications. The meagre economic compensation provides temporarily relief to evacuees but leads to many psycho-sociological and cultural problems of serious nature. The displacement demands change in the lifestyle of people and force them to adjust in a totally alien social milieu. This causes a situation of psychological stress. Compulsory and involuntary displacement together with, 'rarely fair' payment of compensation are its two main reasons as a problem (Menezes 1991). According to him the current system

1. Mental health refer to certain sets of criteria. These are attitudes towards self, which includes accessibility of the Self to Consciousness, Correctness of the self concept, Self acceptance and a sense of identity Growth, Development and Self actualisation, which includes concept of self, motivational processes and investment in living; Integration, which refers to balance of Psychic-forces in the individual, unifying outlook to life and resistence to Stress; Autonomy, which refers to decision-making process, regulation from within; Undistorted Perception of reality including emphathy and social sensivity; Environmental Master including ability to love, adequacy in inter-personal relations and efficiency in meeting situations requirement, capacity for adaptation and adjustment, efficiency in problem solving, adequacy in love, work and play.

fails to acknowledge that an 'oustee' is deprived of a historical right of access to a large number of resources, entire way of life and is not given any opportunity to demand an adequate price for this loss. Apart from his private land and cultural historical heritage, an oustee holds several other livelihood generating assets which are not legally acknowledged. Evidences suggest that these psycho-sociological problems are not well considered, neither by the planners not by those who are the key actors in the implementation of such projects. Therefore, the understanding and management of these problems are more important for effective implementation of these projects.

It is reported that accurate figures of displaced population are not available. Conservative estimate, reveals that around 15 million persons have been displaced from the first to sixth five year plans. The real figure may be as high as 36 millions. Despite the severity of the problems associated with displacement, the country lacks a reliable 'Data base' on the exact situation of displaced people (Vyas 1993). The official sources, by and large, tend to under-estimate the number of persons displaced by developmental projects. For example, different sources reveal different figures of the displaced people from construction of Hirakud Dam as shown in Table 1 (Government of Orissa Report, 1968 and Patanaik, Das and Mishra, 1987).

Table—1

Source	*Dam*	*No. of People Displaced*	*Land Submerged*
Govt. of Orissa Report, (1968)	Hirakud Dam	1.1 Lakh People	1,67,376,83 acres
Patanaik, Das and Mishra, (1987)	Hirakud Dam	1.1 Lakh to 1.6 Lakhs	1,82,592 acres

Displaced Population

The report of the Commissioner for Scheduled Castes and Scheduled Tribes (1990), points out that when the land is acquired and under the present law, only its property form is considered vital questions concerning the very survival of the displaced persons are settled on this basis. Even those, who are identified, are very inadequately compensated. Lack of accurate data on such crucial issues, such as this, is itself an indication of both the Central and State governments degree of concern for the rehabilitation of oustees (Viegas 1987). This current status of displacement is leading to an alarming situation. How to sustain the historical right which the oustee has been deprived off, is an important issue today.

1.2 Rehabilitation and Development

Rehabilitation is more often understood as economic rather than psycho-sociological phenomenon resulting from displacement. It is normally perceived as a 'planned change effort'. In a strict sense it implies, while there is a change the overall effects of the change is to restore the situation to its original condition. In other words change or no change (Franks 1991). Though rehabilitation is sought for development but its nature is quite different from other developmental processes. All developmental efforts imply planned change to improve existing conditions, whereas rehabilitation is designed to restore the status quo. This makes it imperative to understand the term rehabilitation in a much wider perspective, and its components which make it different from other developmental processes.

1.3 Rehabilitation: A Psycho-sociological Perspective

(a) Components of Rehabilitation:

Rehabilitation can be described as having the following components[2].

(i) Antecedent Conditions: Displacement and rehabilitation of people are required when certain 'Antecedent conditions' exist in the situation. For example: National long-term interests for socio-economic development of the country leading to commissioning of various developmental projects; National calamities, such as, war and political turmoil; Natural Disasters, such as, Floods, Earthquakes, Drought and also Man made Disasters.

(ii) Cognitive state of the individuals involved:, i.e., their perception and awareness of the situation, such as:

* Fears and apprehensions about the possible problems to be faced by the affected people.

* Fears and apprehensions about their acceptability by the host population.

---

2. The following format of conceptualisation is partially adopted from the paper, Organisational Conflicts: Concepts and Models by Louis R. Pondy (1967).

* Fears and apprehensions about fulfilment of government promises with respect to providing facilities.
* Attitudes about various "developmental projects" and about "government."

(iii) Affective state of the individuals involved in the situation: Perception of a situation may affect the people in variety of ways such as, developing anxieties. Psychological tension, stress and hostility.

(iv) Manifest behaviour: Psychological effects manifest themselves in variety of behavioural patterns. These range from passive resistence to active resistence, overt aggression and finally agreeing for displacement under stress leading to many other dysfunctional behaviour patterns resulting in poor mental health.

(v) Rehabilitation: Displacement leading to rehabilitation of people through various rehabilitation programmes such as: Allotment of Land: Houses, Monetary compensation, Occupation and many other facilities required for resettlement.

(vi) Further demands by people from government: Any rehabilitation results in an aftermath which manifests itself in further demands by people from government.

(b) Rehabilitation Process:

Drawing upon the ways in which components of rehabilitation are described, it is apparent that, displacement leading to rehabilitation can be described as a dynamic process having definite sequential stages coming one after the other. Each stage has its own characteristics which influences the process in its own way. Displacement leads to deterioration of the situation in the initial states and subsequently to restoration of the situation, quite close to status quo. This is illustrated in Figure I.

Figure I
REHABILITATION PROCESS

Latent Stage
I

Cognitive Stage
II

Affective Stage
III

Manifest Stage, Leading to Displacement
IV

Rehabilitation Stage
V

After-math
VI

Various Stages Depict:

I. Existing State, Antecedent Condition for Displacement
II. Perception/Awareness of the Situation
III. Affects on Individual
IV. Manifest Behavioural Patterns
V. Rehabilitation Programmes
VI. Further Problems/Demands

Rehabilitation process comprises the following six stages:

(i) Latent Stage: It refers to the "Antecedent condition", for example, commissioning of developmental project, leading to displacement and rehabilitation of population. The nature of antecedent condition will determine the ways of handling the situation in terms of "Preparedness measures" and "Coping strategies" by the Government, Other Agencies, Affected People and also by Society. These will influence the characteristic pattern of behaviour of individuals at the next stage, which will also accordingly after the "Preparedness measures and Coping strategies" for the subsequent leading to rehabilitation is characterised by certain stable aspects of condition, perceptions, affects and behaviour discussed later.

(ii) Cognitive Stage: Fears and apprehensions such as:

* Loss of home
* Loss of primary sources of gratification of needs
* Fear of change of basic style of living
* Loss or change in occupation (source of livelihood)
* Fear of adjustment in new jobs
* Loss of social relationships
* Fear of acceptability by the host population
* Lack of confidence in 'Government initiatives' and 'Programmes'.

All the above listed fears and apprehensions are the natural outcomes of displacement and are unavoidable. These must be acknowledged by all concerned. Correct diagnosis of the situation, appropriate 'Preparedness measures' and 'Coping strategies' to minimise them, can greatly reduce the severity of onset of next stage of the rehabilitation process.

(iii) Affective Stage: Perceived fears and threats may or may not affect the people equally under normal circumstances. These come on the surface and show up in various forms, such, anxiety, tension, stress may also lead to hostility. Effective handling of 'affective stage' would accordingly affect the state of next stage of the rehabilitation process.

(iv) Manifest Stage: Degree of psychological tension/stress will greatly influence the behavioural patterns at the manifest stage. People's passive and active resistence to 'evacuating the home land', and demand for better compensation may lead to aggressive behaviour and mass agitation. Quite often they finally agree for displacement under great stress leading to further deterioration of mental health.

(v) Rehabilitation Stage: This stage finally leads to rehabilitating displaced people through various "Rehabilitation Programmes".

(vi) Rehabilitation Aftermath: Howsoever effectively the various stages of rehabilitation process are handled, it will still lead to an 'Aftermath' in terms of further demands by the people leading to increased dependency on the government.

SECTION—B

2.1 Psycho-sociological Consequences of Displacement

It is universally acknowledged that displacement is stressful and sometimes leads to traumatic condition. Inspite of this, the psycho-sociological issues have been neglected in the displacement of people under various projects. Rehabilitation programmes often lack specific components of the aspects of mental health of people. There is no evidence of discussion of the mental health problems and its implications for assessing cost an benefit of development projects.

Here an attempt has been made to discuss in detail the psycho-sociological dimensions leading to mental health problems. It argues that a broadly defined psycho-sociological perspective can have important implications for designing rehabilitation policies. It allows us to anticipate inevitable problems that result from displacement of population to assess the consequence of particular policies.

Systematic analysis of, what happens to individuals, who are subjected to displacement from their homeland and require rehabilitation, will help us to provide the ways and means to minimise the adverse impact of involuntary displacement on mental health of people. Fears and apprehensions discussed earlier are usually perceived as potential threats by the affected population. These are natural and constitute the major components of displacement process resulting in dysfunctional behaviour patterns. These must be considered by all concerned involved in the management of the process. It is imperative to have indepth understanding of the consequences and subsequent careful handling, to minimise their adverse impact on mental health of people. This can be studied at two levels: Individual level and Group level.

Impact at Individual level

(i) Loss or Change in Primary Sources' of satisfaction of Needs: The major fear associated with displacement is, Loss or Change in the primary sources of satisfaction of needs. All behaviours are instigated by needs and are directed towards goals that can satisfy these needs. Personality has a system of organised needs such as (1) Physiological needs; for example, Thirst, Hunger, Sex, (2) Safety needs; for example, Security and order, (3) Social needs; for example, need to belong, Identification and love; (4) Esteem needs; for example need to Achieve, need to control, self respect; and (5) Self-actualisation; for example need for identity and self fulfilment (Maslow 1954). Physiological needs are largely determined by the innate factors but others are greatly influenced by the nature of the social environment. Human beings are constantly seeking for pleasures, reflected through satisfaction of above mentioned needs in their unique manner through their established sources of livelihood, social relations, social status, kinship ties, etc. Any change or blockage, though temporarily, in the manner of satisfying these needs, will result in varying degrees of tension and stress in different people. Therefore, social environment together with the satisfaction of needs in an acceptable manner become extremely important. For example, the satisfaction of the security need which constitutes an important need among the hierarchy of needs in Indian culture is greatly affected by the process of displacement. The compulsive change in the basic style of satisfaction of these needs is usually not welcomed by the people and hence often resisted. People may start pereiving themselves as having low self-worth, 'self-respect' and develop 'negative attitude' towards themselves. In an extreme situation, they may also develop identity crises. All these result in lack of adjustment leading to psychological stress or shock or trauma, as illustrated in FigureII. The major factor associated with this is loss or change in the sources of occupation/livelihood leading to varying degrees of occupational redundancy and loss of social relationships.

(a) Change in Occupation/Livelihood

Fear of change of source of livelihood leads to 'Occupational disruptions'. This may lead to low to high degree of 'Occupational redundancy'. This loss, even if substituted by the new ways managing earning the livelihood, often leads to a state of mental stress. Loss of Agricultural land to the landowners, though given 'Economic compensation' and also new occupational opportunities under various 'Rehabilitation programmes' by the Government could not fulfil the psychological loss such as, social status enjoyed through 'Feudalistic culture', the village leadership leading to psychological satisfaction. All these sources of satisfaction of needs usually get blocked by the relocation process in the new environment.

Loss of land and property is a blow to the oustees, who are unable to secure an alternative source of livelihood because of lack of education and skill. Evidence suggests that many development projects created new occupational opportunities but the people were unable to get the share in the benefits of the project. The displaced persons, by and large, were forced into daily wage labour. For example, the persons displaced by the Pong Dam, who returned to Himachal Pradesh or decided to migrate to other states, in the hope of comparatively more comfortable life, were forced to become landless migrant labourers. Another example is that of 16,080 tribal families from 170 villages displaced by Ukai-Kakarpur Project on river Tapi in Gujarat. Surveys reported that 42 per-cent of all the families, landed or landless were forced to migrate for work for varying periods of time, most of them in the sugarcane factories (Mankodi and Gangopadhyay 1983). All these occupational disruptions, especially loss of job/sources of livelihood lead people to experience feelings of insecurity, defunctness, powerlessness and loss of self confidence leading to stress and in extreme cases to psychological shock. The change in the job in also associated with variety of problems, such as, lack of skill and interest in the new job. Though people are provided training for the new jobs under various Occupational Rehabilitation Programmes, yet they are unable to use their potentials which demotivates them in the new jobs. They also develop feelings of low Self Efficacy (Grist 1987)[3] self Esteem (Brockner 1988)[4], Self Management (Manz & Sims 1980)[5] Self Monitoring (Snyder 1987)[6], and Alienation leading to a great stressful situation.

(b) Loss of Social Relationships

Displacement also forces individual change the pattern of social relationships, Individuals have to undergo an entire process of resocialisation and adjustment in a new social milieu. This leads to loss of existing social relationships. Kinship ties which are important sources of individual's gratification of social needs and in no way less important for an individual's survival. Evidence also suggests that the oustees are sometimes rejected by the parent group. The hostile behaviour of host population further makes the resocialisation difficult for the oustees. Having faced rejection by the parent group and unacceptance by the host population. The oustees go through a tremendous psychological trauma and face an identity crisis. This sometimes leads people to go for second displacement, as in the case of Pong dam oustees (MARG 1987).

(ii) Compensation Package: Inadequate or inappropriate compensation package also results in psychological tension/ stress among the oustees. It has been reported that adequate or inappropriate compensation packages to the oustees have also resulted in lot of psychological stress for the people. The illiterates found it difficult to utilise the compensation amount appropriately. This has led to social evils like alcoholism, gambling and prostitution (Advani 1990).

---

3. Self Efficacy: Individual's belief that he is capable of perform task in a new situation.
4. Self Esteem: Like or dislike themselves, expectations for success leads to risk taking.
5. Self Management: Ability to manipulate Stimuli, Internal Process and responses to achieve personal behaviour outcomes.
6. Self Monitoring: Ability to adjust his behaviour to external situational factors (capacity for adaptation).

Impact at Group Lavel

Displacement also results into disintegration of family, other social groups and occupational groups. Evidence from Augucha Mines of Hindustan Zinc Ltd., at Bhilwara, Rajasthan suggests that providing occupation to one representative of each evacuee's family by HZL helped families, but created family tension resulting in breaking of joint family system and difficulties in setting match in their own community for their children (Advani 1990).

All these psycho-sociological factors discussed above, results into psychological tensions, stress, hostility, sometimes leading to trauma. These get manifested in variety of dysfunctional behaviour leading to mental ill health and sometimes to mental sickness.

SECTION—C

Management of Displacement and Rehabilitation Process

In order to achieve the efficacy of various objectives of resettlement and rehabilitation projects, minimising the adverse effects of displacement must form the primary focus. The success of these projects depends upon, how effectively the displacement is managed and the various rehabilitation programmes are perceived, as appropriate and adequate sources of gratification of needs by the affected population. This makes it imperative to plan, design and implement strategies as 'Preparedness Measures' and 'Rehabilitation Programmes', to cope with negative aspects of displacement, at the appropriate stages of the Rehabilitation Process.

Need for a 'National Policy'

Recognising the adverse impact on human beings, the sufferings and hardships caused by involuntary settlement, the World Bank Policy states as its first requirement, that "whenever feasible, the involuntary resettlement must be avoided or minimised and alternative developmental solutions must be explored (Cernea 1988)." Notwithstanding this policy, there have been cases, when projects have been designed and approved without examining such possible alternatives. Lack of provision of psycho-sociological consideration in the Land Acquisition Law 1894 and also 'Land Acquisition Amendment Act 1984, further weakens the impementation of the Bank Policy. Though rehabilitation has normally been envisaged as a planned change effort, evidences suggest that implementation of each project, called for an adhoc policy of its own. The Bank Policy can be made effective only, if a well-defined 'National Policy' is designed. Introducing psycho-sociological perspective in the Land Acquisition Law will also greatly enhance the efficacy of bank policy. Therefore, the need for a well-defined national policy is a first pre-requisite for effective implementation of resettlement and rehabilitation projects.

Strategies for Minimising Psycho-Sociological Consequences of Resettlement at Various Stages of Rehabilitation Process

(a) Latent Stage

Nature of "Antecedent condition" determines the ways and means of managing resettlement and rehabilitation process. Preparedness measures and coping strategies, need to focus around the factors leading to displacement and their counter impact on population. The rehabilitation process must be pursued with a Developmental Objective rather than merely as coping mechanism in the situation. All preparedness measures and coping strategies at each stage of the process, must reflect the achievement of the developmental objective. These must provide if not better, but almost similar physical amenities and sources of livelihood, by restoring quite close to the *status quo* and then focusing on further development of the people. Therefore, appropriate "interventions" at Government level. NGOs level, Affected Population level and other community level become very important and can make displacement little easier for the people. Figure 3 shows the management of various stages of Rehabilitation process.

(b) Cognitive and Affective Stage

Disastrous Psychological effects on people start showing up in the population to be displaced in the form of tension and stress even before the actual onset of displacement. Issue of the Evacuation notices to the people for acquiring the land is the beginning of the psychological problems of the people degree of stress and tension which the people experience at this stage, because of inherent fears and threats, should be the focus for designing management strategies. Therefore, reduction of this state of tension and stress become extremely important.

Appropriate Preparedness measures needed to be designed at this stage are as under:

Preparedness Measures

Preparedness measures must focus around issues like:

(i) Prepare individuals psychologically to agree for displacement without much resistance.

(ii) Dissemination of timely information about displacement.

(iii) Minimising adverse impact on people.

Conscious efforts at all levels are required to formulate motivational strategies, around perceived potential fears and threats by the people. The following 'Operational Interventions' are needed at this stage:

Operational Interventions

(i) Detailed Microlevel Planning: Detailed Planning in advance, before the onset of displacement, should necessarily form an integral part of the process. The government must procure the data regarding the following aspects about the population to be displaced.

Figure 3
Management of Rehabilitation Process

Well Defined National Policy	Latent Stage-I	Antecedent Condition *Acquisition of Land Leading to Displacement
Preparedness Measures Objectives	Cognitive Stage II	Perception/ Awareness of Situation
* Preparing Individuals of Displacement		
* Dissemination of timely information about displacement		* Fears and Apprehension About
		* Possible problem
* Minimising adverse impact on people		* Fulfilment of Government promises
Operational Interventions		* Acceptability of host population
* Detailed micro level planning		* Attitudes about development projects
* Communication Strategy * People's Participation		
Role of Govt/NGO's/Other Agencies Community and Host Population	Affective Stage III	Developing * Anxiety * Physiological Tension * Stress * Hostility * Shock/Trauma
Management Strategy	Manifest Stage IV Displacement	Behavioural Patterns

* Negotiations with government, Affected people, local leader's other influential people of the area and NGO's * Taking help from: Social research organisations and other agencies for conducting social survey.	Rehabilitation Stage-V	* Passive Resistance * Active Resistance * Overt Aggression leading of mass agitation * Agreeing of displacement under stress
* Rehabilitating displaced	Rehabilitation Atermaths Stage VI	

* Correct estimate of land to be acquired.
* Number of households/families to be displaced.
* Housing pattern of the area.
* Population structure of the place: Adults; males, females; children and old people.
* Caste structure of the area.
* Educational profile of the people.
* Professional skills available with the people.
* Aptitudes and potentials available with the people.
* Correct estimate of movable and immovable property with the people.
* Schools/hospitals, temples, transport and other facilities available to the people in the area.
* Attitude of the host population to know acceptability of the displaced population.

The services of research organisations and other agencies can be of immense help in this regard.

All this data will provide the guidelines to decide the nature of compensation package and facilities to be offered to the people. It will also enable the government to design appropriate communication strategy to create a desirable impact over the people in generating positive outlook about displacement.

(ii) Communication Strategy: Communication strategy should have the following objectives:

* Developing awareness among individuals about need for displacement.
* Providing knowledge about the rehabilitation package and its commitment benefits to people.
* Preparing individuals psychologically to cope up with the unwanted psychological stress.
* Preparing host population for accepting the displaced people.

(iii) People's participation: People's participation should be the core managing technique in designing as well as implementation of communication strategy. All castes, different occupational groups; local leaders and other influential people who are key actors in day-to-day functioning of the affected area, should represent in the rehabilitation process. Resettlement and rehabilitation plans about site for resettlement of people, housing pattern, compensation packages and other facilities should be drawn in consultation with the core participative group. People's involvement would enable the government to elicit commitment and would make the displacement less uncomfortable for people.

Procuring all this data from the people before the onset of displacement can provide a glimpse of government's sincere intentions and efforts of rehabilitating the people after displacement. This will have a positive impact on people and would considerably reduce the adverse affects of displacement.

(c) Manifest Stage

Careful and timely handing of cognitive and affective stage through appropriate preparedness measures would greatly reduce the psychological tension and stress generating dysfunctional behaviour at the manifest stage. In many cases the government has taken an undue long time in deciding the compensation package, forcibly evacuated the people and acquired the land. Evidences suggest that people have shown their actual resistance and resorted to mass agitation under certain development projects. Such a situation can be effectively handled through negotiations between government and affected population. All infrastructural facilities such as land, houses, schools, hospitals, etc. should be provided to people before displacement. This would help in minimising resistance.

(d) Rehabilitation Stage

Rehabilitation programmes necessarily need to be designed according to the felt needs of the affected population. Data about population, procured earlier as preparedness measures must be appropriately used for designing the programmes.

Rehabilitation programmes should make use of available skills and talents and also focus upon providing new skills and competencies to the affected population, to equip them to face the outer world. Efforts should be to develop settler's commitment to self-support and sustenance to avoid onset of settlers dependency syndrome psycho-therapeutic/health programmes in the form of family counselling stress reducing exercises, community programmes and other socio-occupational programmes should form an essential complement of the rehabilitation package along with adequate compensation package. The perception of compensation place, as adequate and good, is greatly influenced by, how effectively the psychological tension, stress and traumatic situation is handled through these programmes.

(e) Rehabilitation Aftermath

Effective management of earlier stages will greatly reduce the further demands by the people from the government.

Conclusion

The paper presents a broad descriptive framework for understanding and managing the neglected psycho-sociological perspective of rehabilitation. The population which is more often displaced by the developmental projects usually belong to lower strata of society, such as Scheduled Castes and Scheduled Tribes who are more affected as compared to other displaced population. Therefore, as a part of socio-economic development, it must concern with safeguarding the interests of minority, the affected population, and minimising the negative impacts of relocations.

Inspite of intentions of the government to provide a comfortable rehabilitation to the affected population, no attention has been paid to the psycho-sociological consequences associated with the process. Though rehabilitation projects are often viewed as a planned change effort with developmental objectives, they are rarely implemented in a manner to achieve those objectives. People have been made to evacuate from their land forcefully and have been made to experience psychological shocks, undergo trauma, more often resulting in mental illness. In fact, if these psychological consequences are not effectively handled, perhaps new resettlement colonies created under the so-called development projects, having objectives of overall development of people for better quality of life leading to national development will, turn into mental asylums. It is, therefore, the right time to reflect on this problem and seriously evaluate the extent to which the policies, planning and strategies together, with its implementation by the government, have been inadequate and draw lessons for further action.

All managers, who are responsible for managing rehabilitation of people and concerned community must appreciate and understand the complex psycho-sociological nature of displacement. Rehabilitation must be addressed as a planned changed efforts having sequential stages requiring detailed advance planning for each stage. Steps are need to arrest the psychological consequences resulting at each stage. This requires correct diagnosis, designing and implementing appropriate interventions as preparedness measures and coping strategies.

This paper began by stating lack of data on the management of mental health issues resulting from displacement and rehabilitation. As such, efforts made in this paper provide guidelines for understanding mental health problems and action strategies for coping with the problem. It is believed that the perspective presented and guidelines suggested in the paper are functional and would be able to solve many of the deficiencies of the current management approach to problems associated with displacement and rehabilitation.

References

1. Advani, Mohan, Socio-economic Aspects of Resettlement and Rehabilitation: A Study of Rampura Augucha Mines, Udaipur, Samaj-Shastra. Hindi Karya Samiti, 1990.
2. Brockner, J.; Self Esteem at Work, Lexington: MA, Lexington Books, Chapt. 1—4, 1988.
3. Cemea, Michael, M.; Involuntary Resettlement in Development Projects, World Bank Technical Paper Number 80. Washington: World Bank, 4, 1988.
4. Commissioner for Scheduled Castes and Scheduled Tribes. Twentyninth report of the Commissioner for SC and ST, New Delhi: The Manager of Publications, Government of India, 245, 1987—89.
5. Franks, Toms. Institutional change and Project Rehabilitation, Hardware, Software and Liveware, in Project Rehabilitation in Development Countries, ed. by Colin, Kirkpatrick, London: Routledge 213, 1991.
6. Gist, M,E.; Self Efficacy: Implementation for Organisation Behaviour and Human Resource Management, Academy of Management Review, 472-85, July, 1987.
7. Government of Orissa. Report on the Benefits of Hirakud Irrigation: A Socio-economic Study, Cuttack: Bureau of Statistics and Economics, Government of Orissa, 13, 1968.
8. Jahoda, Marie, Current Concepts of Positive Mental Health, Joint Commission on Mental Illness and Health, Monograph Series, No. 1, New York: Basic Books, 1958.
9. Mankodi, Kashyap and Tanushree, Gangopadhyay; Rehabilitation: The Ecology and Economic Costs, Surat: Centre for Social Studies, 81, 1982.

10. Manz. C.C. and H.P. Sims; "Self management as a substitute for leadership: A social learning theory perspective. Academy of Management Review, 361-67, 1980.
11. MARG, Pong Dam Oustess; New Delhi, Multiple Action Research Group (Mimemo), 1987.
12. MARG; The Land Acquisition Act and You. New Delhi: Pauls Press, 1990.
13. Maslow, A.H; Motivation and Personality. New York, Harper and Bros., 1954.
14. Menezes, Arul; Compensation for Project Displacement: A New Approach, Economic and Political Weekly, 26 (3), 2465-2469, 1991.
15. Narayan, Sachindra; *Indian Anthropology* New Delhi, Gyan Publications.
16. Narayan, Sachindra; *Dimensions of Development of Tribal Bihar* New Delhi, Inter India Publications.
17. Narayan, Sanchindra; *Sauria Paharia: A Dwindling Tribe of Bihar* Calcutta, Naya Prakash.
18. Patnaik, S.K., B. Das, and A. Mishra; Hirakud Dam Project: Expectation and Realities, in PRIA (ed) People and Dams, New Delhi. Society for Participation Research in Asia, 47-59, 1987.
19. Pondy Louis, R. Organisation Conflict: Concept and Models. Administrative Science Quarterly, 12 (2), 296—320, 1967.
20. Snyder, M.; Public Appearances/Private Realities: The Psychology of Self-Monitoring. New York: W.H. Freeman, 1987.
21. Viegas, Philip; The Hirakud Dam Oustees: Thirty Years after. New Delhi: Multiple Action Research Group (Mimeo), 1987.
22. Vyas, H.N.; Displacement, Compensation and Rehabilitation: A Study of Submergence Area Evacuees, Ph. D. Thesis in Sociology, Udaipur, Mohanlal Sukhadia University (unpublished), 1993.

7

Processes and Experience of Research Method and Techniques at the Micro Level

As I mentioned at the very outset that it is exactly three decades now of doing field work and writing reports; therefore in order to illustrate my hypothesis that the anthropology: The Science of Man in its totality in order to augment itself for 21st century needs to chisel its field techniques and research methods. I will begin with my experience of undertaking first anthropological field work till date. I do not know how much I will succeed but I am trying to present the facts honestly and scientifically.

In the year 1966, I undertook field work in a tribal village known as 'Anjan' in Lohardaga district. It was a part of my B.A. Hons. degree in Anthropology. One teacher was with us to train us in the research methods and field technique in the field situation. The duration of the field work was of four weeks. We were thoroughly trained in participant observation method, genealogical tables, various kinds of conducting interview, photography, etc. We were trained in establishing rapport. The data collected during the day hours were discussed, corrected and suggestions were given in the late evening hours. It necessary the field supervisor were accompanying us and he was giving demonstration of observation method, interview method, life history method, etc., thus we were conducting the actual observation, interview, life history, case study, etc. This continued for a month. On return from field work we were trained for tabulating and analysing the field data and then to prepare the research report. I prepared report on Economic observation of Anjan.

While student of M.A. in Anthropology I presented a research paper on Tribals of Anjan which was very much appreciated. Again I did field work for six weeks as a requirement of M.A. degree in Anthropology. This time field work was conducted in rural setting. This time again field supervisor was there and once again we were going through the rigorous training in research methods and techniques in field situation. We were maintaining field diary daily very meticulously. At that time (in 1967) I was not oaring much for the daily field diary but today whenever I go through those diary I find how useful it was in training us in field observation method which is considered to be the speciality of anthropological study.

Even today in the syllabus the field training is there as requirement of B.A. Hons. and M.A. degree but in real situation teachers are not taking interest largely because of lack of commitment among teachers and the students do not take it seriously because of lack of opportunity of employment in Anthropology. If necessary attention is not paid by the concerned authorities in augmenting the degree of Anthropology with field work, the tradition of field work in the real situation in anthropolgy may dwindle.

Now I will narrate my experience of conducting field work for doctoral level research. After completing my degree of M.A. in Anthropology, I joined the post-graduate department of anthropology in the University of Ranchi. Just after finishing the examination of M.A. I started working on a research project on student unrest in Chotanagpur. The schedule were constructed and printed and we had to collect the data. The last page of the schedule was that of observation sheet. One page was for participant observation report and the other sheet was for recording data based on non-participant observation method. The data were properly collected and observation sheets were duly filled in. We checked the schedule and the observation sheets twice.

Then I started teaching in the Post-graduate Department of Anthropology. After few months I got fellowship for my Doctoral level research of UGC. I did library work for three months, discussed the problem with my supervisor Prof. L.P. Vidyarthi. Each day he gave me one hour time for a fortnight. Then the synopsis for Doctoral research was drafted. My supervisor went through this synopsis very meticulously and incorporating his suggestions the synopsis was finalised and submitted to university for registration for Ph.D. degree went to field for a fortnight and returned with basic data. On the basis of this preliminary field visit a schedule-cum-interview guide and observation sheets were framed. In observation sheet also I jotted down the points which were not to be missed on any account.

This schedule-cum-interview guide and the observation sheets were discussed with the supervisor. His suggestions were also incorporated. I went to field with equipping myself with all required research tools. I stayed in the field for those months. My Ph.D. supervisor also came to supervise me in the field situation. He stayed for four days with me. He went through the data which I had collected before his arrival. He made some suggestions. He also accompanied me for two days in field situation when he got satisfied, he went back. After completing the first leg of field work of three months I also returned. Did sample tabulation and analysis of the collected field data. Discussed these data with the supervisor. After a month again I went to collect the field data for three months. This time supervisor did not come. After three months of once again returned to University. This time I stayed for four months. Then I went to field again for almost four months. This was the final phase of field work. This time I collected all required genealogical tables, case studies, life history, photography and finally said good by to my respondents. Some of the respondents of this field work are so attached that even today I get letter from them. Occasional and ceremonial exchange of visits are also taking place.

After completing my doctoral level research I was asked by my supervisor to work as supervisor of another similar research on Kashi. But before I forget I want to raise here two issues for doctoral researches being done in India today. The above detail suggest that the Ph.D. supervisors were taking much interest in training, guiding and shaping the Ph.D. scholars research aptitude. The students were equally receptive and responsive. I will not say anything about todays Ph.D. supervisors and students of university who are producing each year more than a dozen Ph.D. After 1974, I do not have a chance to work in the university, therefore, whatever I will write will be hear say for which I as an anthropologist have not been trained. Here in the research Institutes we are still trying to maintain the tradition of field work so far anthropology is concerned. I am fully aware that if the Ph.D. scholars are not trained, guided and shaped as per the requirement of anthropology the future of anthropology will be doomed. My experience as a supervisor of the research project is that the role of supervisor is that of a middleman. He has to manage the research and man (research personnel) and sometime the skill of management is to be demonstrated between project director and research assistant. The greatest drawback of large scale research project in social science is the lack of consistency. The person who formulated the hypothesis has no time to supervise the field work and in real situation in most of the cases report is written on the basis of cooked data.

Then I undertook field work in Bodh Gaya independently as an anthropologist. The work of this field work is published in the book form, i.e., Bodh Gaya, Buddha or Shiva. Being an anthropologist I wanted to study the Great Bodh Gaya temple in holistic perspective. I did the preliminary work. When the preliminary field work was in progress I got an appointment letter of scientist in the Space Applications Centre, Ahmedabad. Since this field work was being done on my own, therefore, I decided to complete the preliminary field work and to join the offered position. Decided to complete the work latter on.

I joined the Space Applications Centre, Ahmedabad as a Scientist. Here the main responsibility was to plan, conduct and to prepare report on the Satellite Instructional Television Experiment (SITE) programme. Our responsibility was limited to social and cultural input of the SITE programme. The Scientist to look after the satellite inputs were engineers and other experts of natural science. We were properly oriented and trained in the field of satellite and Instructional research programme. None of the social scientist had the experience of working on this kind of scientific and technical programmes. This was the first such programme in the country. Fortunately most of the social scientists were Anthropologists by training. The tool for conducting the field work was constructed by the experts of the field and data was collected accordingly. In addition to collecting field data through survey method, the holistic method was also widely used by appointing two anthropologists in two different villages of each SITE states. The constant field supervision and logistic support were provided by the senior scientists.

All the scientists sat together for three days and discussed the items of the instruments and then framed the questions in national perspective. The instrument was pre-tested in each SITE states. The data collected during pre-testing was discussed and analysed. The instrument considering the colloquent dialect of each SITE states were prepared. The research instruments were framed according to the requirement of the SITE programme and was duly printed. The research personnel were trained at different levels for data collection, tabulation and analysis of the data.

The experiment was completed successfully. When the experiment was at the end of its completion, some snag developed between technocrats and the social scientists. Barring chief of the social science and one of his assistant all were terminated without any scientific valid reason in the top scientific institution, of the country. Later on the reports were prepared with the help of the consultants. See, this way the researches in social science in India is carried on.

After this SITE research I decided to complete my project on Bodh

Gaya. This I did on my own. I prepared the research design, research tools and also collected data and also did the library work. During this period I was selected as fellow of the Indian Institute of Advanced Study to work on this project time only. But in the mean while I got an offer from A.N.S. Institute of Social Studies. I joined this Institute considering the academic autonomy.

I took a study on Tribals Participation in Panchayati Raj. This was the first study for me to understand the tribals of Bihar through their political institutions, I prepared a set of questions and went for pre-testing, stayed for a week in the field and returned with the data. On the basis of the pre-testing an interview guide-cum-indepth schedule was prepared. Then I went for data collection, stayed for six weeks in the field, returned with field data, tried to find out the gaps in the data. Revisited in the field, stayed for six weeks, collected all relevant data. In the second visit, most of the case studies were collected regarding executive and judiciary functions of the Panchayati Raj system. A detailed interview guide was prepared to interview the tribal and non tribal villages, tribal and non tribal *mukhiyas,* government officials associated with statutory Panchayats, superseded Panchayat Samitis and Zila Parishad, the Gram Panchayat supervisors, Block Development Officers, the District Panchayat Officers, the deputy director and the director of Panchayati Raj. Some were interviewed in groups and others individually. They were selected on random basis, where ever available the cases disposed of by the *gram kutcherries* has been also recorded.

Then I did a study of tribal children: a case study of Oraon to get an idea of Oraon children and their social milieu. It will highlight the educational, social and recreational dimensions of their life. The data for this study was collected from the Barambe village of the Mandar block of the Ranchi district. It lies on Ranchi-Gumla road, 12 miles from the city of Ranchi. I stayed in Barambe only.

Barambe has been selected because one of the oldest Dhumkuria of Oraon is located here. It would be possible to study the traditional method of imparting education through the Dhumkuria. The children, parents, teachers, medical practitioners of different types, a few important villagers like *mukhiya* and Block Officials were interviewed on an interview guide. Then I undertook a study on Sauria Paharia: a primitive tribe of Bihar in development perspective. A pilot survey was undertaken in May 1980 to locate the distribution of Sauria Paharia in the district of Santhal Pargana. Later on the Berio block was selected owing to predominance of Sauria Paharia population. After the selection of block we visited some village of

Berio block and selected Karampahar, Lodohi, Chotapachrukhi, Barapachrukhi and Pachgarh for this study. The cluster of these five villages are fairly representative of the Sauria Paharia population. The Sauria Paharia of Karampahar are more exposed to government officials and non-tribal people than those of Pachrukhi. People from the cluster villages attend the biweekly market in Sahebganj. The Paharias of these villages receive royalty for Sabaigrass and Tendu leaves.

Besides, the Sauria Paharia the personnel involved in the development of the Sauria Paharia through Government and voluntary agencies, local, social and political workers were interviewed indepth with the help of a schedule-cum-interview guide. Genealogical tables, life history matrix, participant and nonparticipant observation, etc. were used to collect the field data.

Initially the Sauria Paharia were hostile but continuous stay in the field reduced it considerably. Good rapport with them enabled us to complete the field work in time.

Then a study on rural development was taken up in which our focus was on developmental inputs induced in Rural Bihar for the development of rural women. This is based on the study of two units of Mahila Vikas Sangh, (MVS), i.e., Tillothu Applique Centre and Mahila Vikas Sangh. I am reproducing here from my book the paragraphs which I wrote for research methods used in this study and at the end. I will record my observation which is update.

The data was collected in the field during January-February 1985. The data has been organised to present the bench mark reports of Tillothu Applique Centre, a unit of the Mahila Vikas Sangh. Apart from bench mark data, the report also discusses the role that the applique centre is playing in enhancing the socio-economic conditions of the women of the rural Bihar. Thus, it is essentially a bench mark survey as well as an impact study. The data collected from field was duly tabulated and analysed. Data from secondary sources were also compiled.

The data was collected with the help of group and individual interview, observation sheets, indepth interview guide-cum-schedule, secondary sources and participant observation method. The research method used for the parent organisation, Mahila Vikas Sangh I wrote. Being an anthropologist I used participant as well as nonparticipant observation method, group as well as individual interview technique. I also went through the records of the MVS as well as of its associates organisations for the purpose of this study. Some of the government officials associated with these programmes were also interviewed for the purpose of data collection.

The field work was of fifteen days, the tabulation and report writing took another fifteen days. considering time and resource constraint I could not do indepth case study which I feel is essential for this kind of study. In the absence of any bench mark survey done prior or just at the commissioning of the programme by the MVS became a great hindrance in preparing this report.

The methodology adopted in this study is different from earlier studies because the anthropologist has now to diagnose and prescribe the prescription quickly. The services of the anthropologist are quite often required for short-term planning. This is so because in most of the international loan or grant their is a clause of submission of report by anthropologist or social scientist. Therefore, this kind of mandatory or obligatory research has given birth to a quick appraisal research, whenever required for this kind of research. I am using the above mentioned research methods and techniques.

At the threshold of 21st century when developed Man is trying to buy flat in space and the primitive and dwindling tribe with their barter economy is trying hard for survival is the real subject of anthropological laboratory. Anthropology has to study both and therefore anthropological methodology needs to be properly equipped for undertaking study of the Man of the two extremes. The fundamental research methods are fundamental in nature and hence it needs to be polished according to the scientific requirements of the 21st century.

Earlier social science like History, Philosophy, etc. were not any research methods for data collection, they were depending solely on secondary source of data. But now in these social sciences the data is collected from the field, from primary sources and therefore are using almost all research methods which were earlier used only in the Anthropology. Research method like genealogical method which was coined and used exclusively in Anthropological study is now being used widely in the History and constructing and reconstructing oral traditions. There are many departments in the universities of USA where anthropological methods are widely used in other social sciences.

The holistic approach, the genealogical tables and the participants observation were considered essentially anthropological research method in which anthropologists were trained and oriented but today these are widely used in others social sciences. Thus, considering the use of these research methods in various social sciences we ought to consider and reconsider for anthropological research methods.

Further the canvas of anthropological researches has changed and extended. Now each social phenomenon to which Man is associated is being studied. The dimension and the dynamics of anthropology is extended and is under the process of change and continuity. Hence, the research methods equally needs to be extended and to be under the process of change and continuity. Anthropology is studying now the primitive Man to space Man. Generally by adding some more research technique inputs we study space MAN. For studying MAN of space we ought to have a suitable research technique where addition is not sufficient and scientific. So is the case with the physical anthropology or linguistic anthropology or prehistory and anthropology, etc.

Since the laboratory of the anthropology is global and the Man of the global level is changing fastly, therefore the research methods for studying fast changing Man at the global level also needs to be properly equipped unless we do design required change or modification or addition in existing research methodology the data collected for such studies from existing methodology will not be that scientific and accurate as it should have been. The anthropologists who will be entering to 21st century shortly, specially the young anthropologists, should sit together and discuss the research methodology based on their research experience and their projected need of 21st century research. Such discussion at the global level will be quite useful and will result into modified and added research methods. It is not that the Man of 21st century will suddenly change their physical characteristics but the social and cultural characteristics are changing fastly. The social institutions are eroding, the values are changing, the world view and ethos perspectives have equally been effected. The changes taking place are almost changes, it is not gradual. In order to understand and to study this kind of social phenomenon of 21st century we need to have accordingly well equipped research methodology.

In the second part of this article which I would be writing after returning from USA and 14th ICAES will deal with concrete research models and designs based on my experiences and discussions with the anthropologists of the different countries of the world.

8

Perspectives of World Anthropology with Special Reference to Indian Anthropology and Gandhian Approach of Development

Anthropology has been on the march through the ages. The 'Child of Darwin' as Merret called it, in a way, celebrated its centenary with the Origin of Species in 1859. It took, however, a considerably long time to get it professionally institutionalised on the global plane when the British anthropologists took the initiative to organise the First Institutional Congress of Anthropological and Ethnological Sciences in London in 1934.

The 21st century has been declared as the century of Anthropology. The present study has been undertaken with the four specific objectives. First, to reflect on the accomplishments and lessons of the past 100 years of anthropology; second, to examine the challenges of anthropology in the new millennium and third, to explore the application of insights of anthropology to public policy, education, business and human services. There are many anthropological 'realities' produced and reproduced in the local and global systems of thought and knowledge which needs to be understood, analysed and properly documented. Fourthly, the Gandhian approach of development. Mahatma Gandhi had his own approach for the development of ten tribes. As the result of his impact on tribe, we find today TANABHAGAT, which is a detailed study on them.

Indian Anthropology reflects the diverse problems of the Indian social system. Indian Anthropology owes its origin to the Asiatic Society of Bengal, which was established in 1774 by Sir William Jones to study "nature and man". Since last two hundred twenty-five years, Indian Anthropology has marched ahead and attempts have been made by anthropologists in the past viz., Roy (1922), Dubey (1962), Bose (1963), Majumdar (1950, 1956), Vidyarthi (1966, 1978) and Narayan (1988) to classify the course of development in terms of dominant trends in anthropological investigation. While it was too early for S.C. Roy (1922) to classify the ethnographic studies in terms of time perspective, he simply categorised them in terms of the sources of publications, i.e., magazines, handbooks, monographs, etc. He also attempted to identify the nationality of the authors who conducted investigation among the different tribes and castes in India. However, the attempts of Majumdar (1956), Vidyarthi (1978) and Narayan (1988, 1996), were quite significant Borrowing the terms of T.K. Penniman (1935), D.N. Majumdar for the first time divided the anthropological researches in India into phases which was further reclassified, reanalysed and redefined by Vidyarthi (1978) and Narayan (1996). Thus, at the close of century I wish to reflect on the accomplishments and lessons of the past 100 years of anthropology.

Secondly, the challenges of anthropology at the threshold of 21st century is great. Anthropology is no longer confirmed only to the study of the primitive societies rather important role of anthropologists is to research and advise on the impact of technology and innovations, the personal or social consequences of planned change and 'development' or of 'progress', such studies seek to protect and enhence the welfare and quality of life of those most vulnerable to the impact of technology and innovations those among whom these are introduced and promoted. Their information can also be to often or direct, redirect or prevent the undesirable consequences of innovations, in the hope of enabling the survival of people in society worth inhabiting.

Study of change, may be rural or tribal or urban, continues to be favourite field of study for anthropologists. Anthropological studies differ from other studies by economists, political scientists and journalists in the sense that the anthropologists use more scientific methods such as participants observation which is considered to be an essential element of social anthropology aiming to get intimate and first-hand information about the subject.

Development is the most illusive and important concept in the Indian science. My research experience of last three decades suggest that the people of India by and large have been deceived in the name of development. Development for whom and development for what must be addressed otherwise it remain only a popular cheap political slogan. At the threshold of 21st century, it is being felt than the concept of development needs to be redefined.

Almost five decades of planned development targetted to Indian population is going to be completed soon but the achievement are at dismay. Of course, certain group of tribes of India, urban or rural population of India got benefited but in turn they are playing the role of middleman in amassing a huge amount of wealth in the name of development. Rather a small section of population of tribal or rural or urban India has extended helping hand in exploiting their own men. The exploiters are nexious of politicians and bureaucrats. This dimension of development needs to be highlighted. This is the darker side of the development helping the growth of black money and criminalising the bureaucratic and political set-up of the country which in turn has divided the Indians in small selfish groups in the name of caste/subcastes/religion/political affiliation/class affiliation.

Mahatma Gandhi never dream of this kind of India. The socialist/ rightist or leftist thinkers of India never desired for this kind of India. But today what we find is disgusting. Youth are ready to kill youth in the name of reservation in job opportunity. Reservation was initially designed for limited period but it is continuing and you can found all kind of devil's activity to get a certificate for reservations in job opportunity where the country is being drifted in the name of development. Should we allow this kind of development to continue or should we go for an amendment in our constitution.

The politicians without understanding the meaning of development become chief designer and implementer of development. The result is before us. The Gandhian approach to development of the tribals and rural people of India is quite relevant and deserves not only our concern but also requires to made a nodal point for development. Gandhiji was not an intellectual in the academic sense of the term but his thinking had the quality of creative genius. He was pre-eminently a man of action. He has written a great deal but his writings are designed as a guide to action and not for the acquisition of knowledge. They are generally concerned with the solution of his actual problems arising out of the many sided and complex situation.

Thirdly, to explore the application of insights of anthropology to public policy, education, business and human services. The latest application of anthropology mentioned by Brainschwimmer in current

Anthropology (vol. 37 number 3, June 1996) is on the Internet. The Internet is vast and expanding computer network that has the potential to provide substantial resources for anthropological scholarship with unprecedented rapidity and economy. Of late the anthropological insight to public policy has been realised and due importance is being given to it. The anthropological insight even in planning for genetic engineering nutritional input, environment and ecological imbalance are widely used. The development in the physical quality of man is of prime concern for anthropologists. It also includes the socio-economic moral-ethical values, world view and ethos, etc. The holostic development of the man is the nodal aim of the anthropologists with anthropological insight and excellence. From micro to macro or vice-versa everywhere we find the anthropological insight being used for development. The anthropological research techniques and tools are widely used these days in policy research and development research.

For this study I have some field data and will also be collecting more and will be supplementing it with the interviews of a few eminent anthropologist of USA working of India, a few noted political thinkers on Gandhi, a few noted economist on development and Gandhi, etc. The library work and report writing will be done in the Woodrow Willson centre, Washington, USA. So far no such study has been done, therefore, it is the pioneering study in the field of anthropology. This study will have great bearing on the anthropology of 21st century because of the fact that I am exploring the application of insights of anthropology to public policy, education, business and human services.

9

Rural Development: The Two Models

Rural Development has emerged as a distinctive field of policy and practice and of research. This strategy came to be formulated as a result of the general disenchantment with previous approaches to development planning at national and sectoral levels, and it is defined by its concern with equity objectives of various kinds—specially the reduction of inequalities in income and employment and in access to public goods and services and the alleviation of poverty. It is this focus on distributional issues which has marked out 'Rural Development' as a distinct field, because an overwhelming majority of poor people in the developing countries live in rural areas. The World Bank, indeed recently declined Rural Development as a strategy designed to improve the economic and social life of a specific group of people—the rural poor.

The term Rural Development thus refers to a distinct approach to interventions by the State in the economics of underdeveloped countries. It is, in fact, a distinct approach to the development of the economy as a whole. It is more specific in the sense that it focuses particularly on poverty and inequality.

The expression of Rural Development may also be used, however, to refer to processes of change in rural societies, not all of which involve action by government. In this case the activity of Rural Development a form of State intervention must be considered simply as one of the forces concerned—although it is on which has become of increasing importance.

There was a report by Sri Bunker Roy in Delhi edition of *the Statesmen* of May 9, 1996 on page 9 entitled Grassroots Struggle for a privilege.

Mr. Bunker Roy maintains that "the crucial issue facing the rural poor today in India is very simple. Does a poor illiterate peasant, landless labourer, artisan and rural women have a right to demand from the Government details of development expenditure carried out in their village?

Do they have right to ask for copies of bills and vouchers and names of persons who have been paid wages contained in master rolls on the construction of schools, dispensaries, small dams, and community centres that on paper have been shown to have been completed?

If they are willing to pay for these documents to be photocopied, which could also serve as certified copies in case any police cases have to be registered against village officials or politicians for embezzlement, corruption or misappropriation, can the Government refuse."

In 1990, a mass based organisation called the Mazdoor Kisan Shakti Sangathan MKSS started working with the very poor peasants in an area that is openly acknowledged as one of the worst and most backward regions of Rajasthan-Bhim Tehsil on the borders of the three districts of Pali, Ajmer and Rajsamand. The idea of MKSS was to find out the root problems behind the issue over non-payment of wages to workers on Government projects under the department of forests and Public works.

At every stage they faced obstructions when they asked for information and details of expenditure on schools, dispensaries, drinking water schemes, rural housing dams and community centres. On paper they were shown to be complete but to the whole village it was obvious that some one had misapproriated the funds—school buildings with no roof, dispensaries with no walls, dams left incomplete and community centres with no doors or windows. The MKSS wanted the details everyone knew but no one wanted to say.

As in every Government, there are some bureaucrats who are concerned about funds reaching the poor and be spent wisely and properly. After years of knocking the doors, one young recently recruited IAS officer managed to extract some details from the block office. In order to share this information with the public and with the people of same village (Kot Kirana in Pali district), the MKSS organised the first *Jan Sunwayi* (People's hearing) in the history of Rajasthan. At the outset, the MKSS had insisted it was a hearing and not a court (adalat). Everyone was welcome to listen and respond—a politician, administrator, landless labourer and private contractor—and if they wishes to say something to defend themselves, the MKSS would give them the platform.

Corruption is nothing new. There is no one in the villages in Rajasthan who does not think that the village officials are scoundrels and thieves.

So what is new? What can one Jan Sunway do? By reading the details of the bills and vouchers and names of people, they made it very personal. The audience who can heard the names being read out how led and screamed at the brazenness of the officials and their elected leaders. The response was electrifying and all of a sudden it was no longer a game.

With the phenomenal response from the people to the first public hearing, several other public hearings were organised from December 1994 to April 1995 in the same region.

It was through this process that two demands emerged unanimously from all the public hearings. One, that any citizen from the village should have the right to make photocopies of all bills, vouchers and muster rolls on payment for any work done by the Government in their village. Two, that funds embezzled and misappropriated should be recovered from these village officials and politicians, their property be attached, and assets frozen and publicly auctioned and that the money recovered should be spent back in the same village. No departmental enquiry, no cases be registered - just return the money and let's get on with it.

In April 1995 in an historic announcement on the floor of the State Assembly, the then Chief Minister of Rajasthan declared that any citizen had the right to information. On payment, any one could demand and receive details of expenditure on work done over the past 15 years in their villages and all the documents could be photocopied as evidence should they want to use it in future. Since India's independence, no State Government had ever made such a sweeping commitment and the coverage and vision of the Chief Minister was unanimously applauded.

With the commitment of the Chief Minister on the floor of the House, what had to follow were Government orders...

In a classic but anticipated instance of double speak, typical of Governments an order was hastily issued that very night. It made no mention of the right to photocopy documents but allowed for "inspection" and written details by hand with no coertification possible what the Chief Minister committed on behalf of the Government, the bureaucracy manled and distorted out of sense and content.

In a sense, whatever the outcome, raising the issue of the right to information and demystifying it is a manner that every peasant, industrial worker and landless labourer now understands. The demand for information on development expenditure will increase.

II

The other case study is from Bihar of Manav Vikas Kendra (MVK) a voluntary organisation working among the Mushars of Jagdeeshpur block of Bhojpur district. Sri Mantoshwar. Sinha popularly known as Mantosh Bhai, who left school on the call of J.P. (Sri Jai Prakash Narain) and joined the cadre of Chachatra Sanghasna Vahini at the tender age of 12. He was with J.P. until his death and he says that on the instructions of J.P. he started working among the Mushar of Jagdeeshpur. The area of action programme was also suggested by J.P. Jagdeeshpur, once up on a time in history has a glorious period because of being a place known for Babu Veer Kunwar Singh. It is in the Bhojpur district which is considered to be a disturbed district from law and order point of view. The Naxal activity was also there. These days the region is also known for socio-economic political tension. Though the place has remain a seat of political movement since historical days. Sociologically it has a mixed population. Mrs. Manju, wife of Mr. Mantosh is also an activist. It is an inter-caste marriage arranged by J.P.

Mr. Mantosh and Ms. Manju went to the village and started living with one of the farmer. For six months they did not do anything except to mix with the villagers and teaching children of the village irrespective of caste. When they established good rapport with the villagers then gradually they started meeting with the Mushars. After having complete detail of the Mushar of the each village of the block, they started identifying and contacting such voluntary organisation who can extend their programmes to these Mushahars. Mr. Mantosh worked first of all to raise their economic standard, then to literate them and then to improve their health. In this endeavour after facing a lot of difficulty he achieved little success.

But one thing in which he has succeeded tremendously is the awareness programme. MVK had made each Mushar of his area of operation literate. MVK has made them aware of their rights and duties. MVK is now playing the role of a coordinator between Mushars and Block office. Therefore, each programme meant for them now reaches to them without any extra effort. But even then some 'lapses' and 'gaps' remain their which draws our attention. I presume that the day on which such 'lapses' and 'gaps' will be 'removed' and 'filled' will be a red day in the history of Rural Development.

III

In recent days I have been reading news item, editorial and articles on corruption. It is being presented that a war against corruption has come up. But unfortunately it is not a fact. If we make a content analysis of the most of the published material we find that majority of these are for public relation work. How corruption can be removed when 48 per cent population of the total population is still illiterate. Even after 50 years of the independence of the country we have not been able to provide majority of the population the minimum two meals a day. The drinking water, the minimum health condition and a roof on the head is a far cry.

Awareness of rights and duties of an individual is a pre-condition for the success of any programme. The provisions of the latest Panchayati Raj act if adopted may help in bringing change through rural development programme. These programmes again be made area specific and people specific. The target oriented programmes are the need of the hour. People must have right to information. Today we have isolated case of Rajasthan and a little similar case in Bihar but may be after ten years we will have more such cases. People should not be mistaken. When the people of India become aware they achieve Independence. Our history is full of such examples. From Chanakya to Gandhi we find the similar thing. Gandhi did nothing but except to make the people aware of the rights, duties and prevailing situation.

The two models of rural development presented in this paper suggest that the programmes of rural development needs a careful consideration at the threshold of 21st century. It needs to be considered as a tool of rural development rather than that of a tool of political development. The strong political will shown by the Chief Minister of Rajasthan probably will be of great help in developing the lot of the people residing in the rural areas.

10

Strategies for Solving Energy Problems of Tribal Bihar

In modern world energy holds the key to development as energy consumption is linked with economic progress. Generally, higher income or output of nation is closely related with higher level of energy consumption. However, energy is one element of the infrastructure required for production and the daily needs of masses, which cannot be imported on any scale for a country like India's population and size. So self-reliance and higher degree of self-sufficiency is urgently called for.

The largest consumer of energy in our nation is the household sector, accounting for 50 per cent of total energy consumption in rural areas and most of this derived from non-commercial sources like firewood, animal, plant and agricultural waste, etc. Bulk of the new and renewable sources of energy are sun, wind power, biomass waste utilization, etc. Therefore, there has to be a decentralised planning for Integrated energy sources to satisfy a variety of energy needs. The Integrated Rural Energy Planning Exercise is an effort in this direction to formulate strategy for tackling the problems of energy and improving the quality of life in the rural areas.

Balanced micro regional development has emerged as an important top priority item of national planning programme as 80 per cent of the population of the country lives in villages in condition of abject poverty. With this concept the Planning Commission has evolved an Integrated Rural Energy Planning Programme to uplift the rural people by changing them from energy dependence to energy autonomy. As the programme is of an integrated approach the coordination of various sectors in the development departments are very essential and the success of rural energy planning programme depends on the degree of coordination and linkage with other sectors and the institutions working on developing technologies appropriate to the rural areas.

The plan document had pointed out the seriousness and magnitude of the energy crisis in the rural and tribal areas and had recommended an integrated approach for planning and implementing rural energy programmes.

The IREP programme consists of a central component, 100 per cent grant is being provided to the States/Union territories for setting up State and district/block level IREP cells consisting of professional and support staff. Central funds have also been provided for training of the staff and for extension and other related activities.

The State level funds have been provided in the plan for each State/UT for the IREP programme which is under the budget head of Rural Development.

The IREP projects involves utilising existing schemes for energy supply to rural areas including rural electrification, social forestry, non-conventional energy technologies, kerosene, soft coke, etc. However, items not covered by any of the schemes may also be promoted, subject to availability of funds from the State IREP budget. But this programme is yet to make its dent on tribal population because of obvious reasons and therefore, I wish to undertake this study with the objectives mentioned below.

Rural Energy in Tribal Bihar

The tribal Bihar is rich in natural resources like forest, waterfall, animal wastes and other wastes which can be successfully used for producing rural energy. The leaf and other wastes are found in abundance in tribal Bihar which can be successfully used in producing rural energy. The climate of tribal Bihar is equally suitable for solar energy.

Non-conventional sources such as solar energy, wind energy, bio energy are still not very much developed and so are not in common use. Hence, it become essential to plan the introduction of these non-conventional energy systems for the tribal masses in general and particularly for primitive and dwindling tribe.

Objectives

1. To identify the places where wind energy and bio energy is available in plenty.
2. To suggest how these sources can be used in a better way to provide non-conventional energy to the poor tribals.

3. To train them to become produce of non-conventional energy and an ideal user suiting to their ecology and tradition in various economic agricultural activity.
4. To develop the socio-economic conditions of the tribals through non-conventional energy.
5. To suggest them how to keep environment pollution free through non-conventional energy.

11

Voluntary Association/Organisation/ Non-Government Organisation and Child Labour Elimination Programme in Bihar

An association may be defined as a group of individuals united for a specific purpose or purposes and held together by recognised or sanctioned modes of procedure and behaviour.

The association must be distinguished from the institution, a term now usually referring not to individuals in union but to forms or modes of social relationship. Thus, 'property' is an institution since it is a recognised social relationship in respect to external objects, war is an institution as a method of settling disputes between States. A Trade Union is an association since it consists of individuals grouped for certain purposes sometimes the same term is used to refer both to institution and association, but even then the distinction should be sufficiently clear. For example, the State is spoken of as an institution or rather as a complex of institutions when the reference is to a body of rules or mechanisms defining and maintaining the relation between individuals under a common territorial rule; but a State is also an association since it consists of individuals united for certain very general and pervasive purposes. In other cases no ambiguity arises. Thus, marriage is an institution, a recognised mode of procedure designed to define the relation between sexes but a family or rather a married couple may be regarded as an association.

In psychology the term association is sometimes contrasted with organisation, the former implying mere casual juxtaposition of units and the latter control by a general scheme. This distinction has been applied by Bosanquet to human aggregates but it appears to be one of degree rather than of kind. Both in the case of mental elements and in that of individuals association may be shown to vary in the degree of organic character they possess with the comprehensiveness and depth of the factors upon which they rest. Nevertheless all association implies some degree of organisation, however, rudimentary of transient.

The term purpose used in the description of associations must be understood to cover a wide range of contain and must not be limited to cases of clearly formulated and articulate volition. It should be remembered that even where the chief or dominant purpose of an association is grasped by its constituent members, there are often present their purposes of varying importance which may not be understood by all the members. It is also clear that the purposes of associations are not unitary and that people may join them form quite different and even conflicting motives. Moreover, as is clearly illustrated in the history of bodies like trade unions, the purposes of an association, like those of individuals, undergo change in the process of realisation and the manner in which this change takes place is hardly open to the inspection of the most perspicacious. As Bosanquet insists, associations and institutions have such character that they appear as though instituted to fulfil some purpose. Although they can be understood only teleologically, however, we must not regard them as the embodiment of a unitary mind but rather as trial and error experiments which have grown up through groping and which gradually attend clarity and coherence.

Associations serve specific purposes and therefore embody only partial interests of the individual and consequently of the community. Some associations no doubt are very comprehensive and represent interests affecting large numbers or even as in the case of State all the members of a society. But no single association and not even the whole associational structure of a people can adequately express the infinitely varied, complex and subtle relations which constitute the total integral life of a community and some of the most valuable elements in the line of individuals are outside the scope of effective organisation.

In the study of primitive peoples the term association is used to include units other than those of the kindred and the local group. Recently a tendency has become apparent to lay stress on associations as agencies which lead to unification independently of the ties of kinship which thus have political significance. But Lowie who in his earlier work was inclined to sympathize with this attitude has recently shown that even among primitive peoples associations may constitute disruptive as well as unifying forces and that there is no clear correlation between territorial integration and the presence of associations.

In the historical period the relations between associations and the State have been extremely varied and complex and hardly lend themselves to summary discussion. The medieval guilds, the fraternities for the enforcement of true of God and the communes played an important role in moulding political structure. There are occasions as for example in imperial Rome when corporations which begin as extra political bodies come to have political significance. Instances also abound where the State looks upon associations with suspicion and even endeavours to suppress them as at some periods in French history.

The multiplication of associations is one of the most striking features of modern social life. No adequate classification of them has yet been derived and reliable statistical data are extremely difficult to obtain. Roughly, they may be grouped according to their functions into occupational, religions, cultural and recreational bodies. Empirical thinking of the kind done by the book-keeper and duly refined, by scientist. But he by no means held, as some lesser philosophies, such as Helvetius, seem to have done, that gives the right education and the right social environment, all men can use the gift of reason perfectly; nor did he hold that even the full gift of reason can unlock for those who have it all the mysteries, or solve all the problems, with which the universe confronts men. He summed up his position nicely in a letter written to Le Cati in 1741. That which our eyes and mathematics demonstrate to us, we must hold to be true. In all the rest we must say only; I do not know", (see Gay 1959, p. 26).

Voltaire's political ideas were consonant with his appraisal of ordinary human capacities. He was not a defender of "enlightened despotism"; on the other hand, he was not a very good democrat, if such a democrat must really believe that the many can be trusted to make policy, to guide the State by referenda. In the balance, he leaned toward an almost Fabian hope or trust that an intelligent minority will act as guide—but never as tyrant—and would leave ordinary men reasonably free to behave reasonably well.

Voltaire, then, was in a sense a skeptic, at least in not accepting conventional Christianity or indeed any formal theology or metaphysics; but he was also in a sense a believer, and from his work, along with that of many others, has been built up a world view, a faith that has no church but many followers. All these followers have in common a rejection of traditional sacramental Christianity and its immanent God; many of them are also optimistic, rationalistic, egalitarian, and democratic in a way that Voltaire, whom they almost always revere, was not. Yet one suspects that even today he would not altogether repudiate his children.

Although in his style, and in much of his substance, Voltaire conforms to the stereotype of the French national character current among French and foreigners alike, he has never quite been accepted in France as that essential figure in modern nationalism, the one great writer who is both supremely national and supremely universal. France has no Shakespeare, no Dante, no Cervantes, no Goethe. For so many of his countrymen Voltaire's ecrasez Linfame is still so partisan and so bitter a memory as to deprive him of such a place in the hearts of all his countrymen.

Voluntary Associations (Anthropological Aspects):

An association is a group organised for the pursuit of one interest or of several interests in common. Associations are usually contrasted with involuntary groupings serving a greater variety of ends, such as kin groups, castes, social classes, and communities.

Attention was first drawn to the characteristics and significance of associations in the context of the evolutionary approach to social phenomena. Although the earlier writers took little interest in particular associational forms (a general study made by Heinrich Schurtz in 1902 was an exception), they attributed great importance to the shift from involuntary to voluntary kinds of grouping. Sir Henry Maine stressed the movement from relations based upon status as determined by birth to relations of contract deriving from the free agreement of individuals. Maine thought of early society not only as being based upon kinship but as lacking settled residence. He said that "when a tribal community settles down finally upon a definite space of land, the Land begins to be the basis of society in place of the kinship" (Maine 1875, p. 72). According to this view (latter reiterated by Morgan), territorial association is a new principle of human grouping that makes possible the emergence of the state. Ferdi-n and Tonnies made a similar distinction when he contrasted Gemeinschaft with Gesellschaft; Emile Durkheim and others continued in the same tradition.

Insofar as the concept "association" differentiates certain forms of grouping from others (e.g. castes from clans, its theoretical value lies in the analysis of social evolution. Voluntary associations become more common and significant as societies advance in technology, complexity, and scale; hence, their study is part of the study of social change.

A good illustration of the point at which associations first emerge is provided by the Blackfoot Indians of the North American plains. The Blackfoot's existence was formerly based on hunting the buffalo; as the feeding habits of the buffalo changed from season to season, so Indian life had to change correspondingly. In the autumn and winter when pasture was poor, the buffalo wandered about in small herds. The Blackfoot also travelled about in small bands of kinfolk led by a man chosen for skill in hunting and fairness in his dealings. In late spring the buffalo congregated in enormous herds, flattening on the fresh and abundant grass. The Blackfoot bands also combined, forming social and economic units that could most efficiently hunt the great herds. Most men were members of societies that included men of similar age. These societies organised the encampments, maintained order, and coordinated hunting operations during the summer migrations. The societies also performed dances and ceremonies. Quite apart from the explicit ends served by these associations, they brought men from different bands into relations of solidarity. Although a young man might choose which society he would join, it was hardly conceivable that he should belong to none. In this case the principle of association was compounded with that of age-grouping, and membership was voluntary only in a restricted sense.

In the comparative analysis of social organisation it seems preferable to keep the two principles of grouping separate. Lowie, who did not press this distinction, concluded that the distribution and form of associations were so irregular that they defied logical classification (1948, 1960, p. 295). Nevertheless, a very loose pattern can be observed; among relatively small and technologically primitive groups, associations tend to be organised for recreation and the expression of distinctions of rank; in larger tribal societies they may exercise important governmental functions, and with an increasing division of labour they tend to be founded for the pursuit or defence of economic interests.

Among the Crow Indians, there was a cult organised as an association to undertake the ceremonial planting of tobacco; this was believed to promote the welfare of the tribe. Membership in the Tobacco society conferred prestige and was acquired by paying a substantial fee to a sponsor. Members performed special songs and dances. The various chapters shared the fees of novices. Both men and women might belong, and it was common to initiate a man and his wife at the same time (Lowie 1935). Another example can be taken from the culture of the Banks Islands (Melanesia), in which there were two distinct sets of associations, one secular and one ceremonial. A young man at puberty was initiated into a young man's club (sukwe) if he or his kinsmen paid the required entrance fee. He could afterwards advance to higher ranks within the club by giving costly presents. Initiation could take place at any age, and recruits did not have to start in the lowest rank. The principal functions of these sukwe seem to have been those of fostering sociability and fixing rank. The other associations (tamate) were ritualistic and secret; masks were worn and the meeting places were taboo to women and uninitiated males. No one could pass above a certain rank within sukwe unless he had been initiated into the most important of the tamate societies, but neither society had any direct part in government.

The Ariori society of the Society Islands (Polynesia) included both male and female members. It was numerically strong and divided into a series of ranks. The principal function of the Ariori was to provide public entertainment, but it seems in addition to have been a powerful integrative force in the community. The religious aspect of the ceremonials was also important; members were obliged to kill any new children they might bear, apparently to avoid obligations that might interfere with their Ariori responsibilities (Williamson 1939, pp. 113—153).

Among the Yako in eastern Nigeria there is a pattern of dense settlement with authority concentrated at the level of the local group. Associations of varying kinds were based on both the ward, including about three thousand people, and the village, which could have a population of up to ten thousand. Neither within nor between them was there any explicit hierarchy of authority, although the plurality of associations was remarkable. The maintenance of order ultimately depended on the common understanding and coincident interests of the associations, but because they were based on different groupings and their membership overlapped, consensus was more easily obtained. In each ward there was an association of "leaders", the head of which had moral authority over other men's associations: the "fighters", the "hunters", and a graded ritual association into which most males were initiated. Within each ward there was also an independent association that offered supernatural protection to its members and regarded itself as a means of defense against any abuse of power by the "leaders": it had become a reluctantly tolerated opposition.

The village was a larger unit than the ward and had a cult association with about fifty members, to which ward leaders usually belonged. The head of this village association belonged to a council of priests, which appeared to have begun as a combination of diverse cults associated with matrilineal clans but had become a corporation of considerable solidarity. This council had judicial and deliberative capacities supported by ritual powers and moral authority, but it could not enforce its views. Other village associations had police powers, such as "the body of men" concerned with trespass and the stealing of crops. A body with more prestige, consisting of forty men, was concerned chiefly with land disputes and trading relations. The members were pledged to divulge information on alleged offences to the association and to keep them secret from outsiders. Admission to this association was by succession on the death of a close patrilineal kinsman. The radical decentralisation of authority among the Yako is dependent upon the extensive use of associational grouping in conjunction with double unilineal descent and influential spirit cults (Forde 1961, pp. 309-323).

In West Africa, associations also play an important part in the government of some societies with centralised state like authority, such as the Yoruba in Western Nigeria and the Mende in Sierra Leone. In parts of Yorubaland, the Ogboni association of elders was a judicial body, which in Abeokuta elected and could remove the principal political chief. The Ogboni had at its disposal a society of hunters and scouts who would seize the property of an uncooperative minor offender and a ritual association that carried out executions of criminals. Among the Mende, the Poro society used to be the most powerful organ of government. The functions of the Mende chief were of a secular character, concerned with military and administrative duties; he could be deposed or reproved by the Poro, which controlled all important ritual activities and met in secret. All youths were initiated into the Poro and received training in masculine tasks and morals, but actual authority was limited to the senior members. Other Mende associations exercised authority over particular realms of activity; the Humui supervised sexual behaviour, the Njayei treated insanity, and the Kpa dealt with minor physical disorders. The Sande was a women's society paralleling the Poro, and as the voice of organised feminine opinion it too could be of political importance (Little 1951).

Among other peoples, such as the Ashanti in Ghana, the Dahomey, and the Nupe in northern Nigeria, the central government controlled the use of force and State rituals. For example, among the Ashanti young men's military organisations had a voice in the election of a chief, but in general no important spheres of authority in these societies were left to independent bodies such as associations. Where found, associations usually organised mutual aid and recreation. Saving clubs, widespread, in this region, often had power to regulate the behaviour of their members.

The appearance of associations seems to be linked with new forms of economic activity. Among the Temne in Sierra Leone, for example, the introduction of swamp-rice cultivation created new labour demands for the initial clearing of the swamps and for the annual farming cycle. A secret society was formed for clearing the swamps, and young men's associations were founded to help with the farming. Travelling from farm to farm and working collectively, the young men were able to earn extra money and productivity was much higher (Banton 1957, pp. 20-21, 193-195). Among the Yoruba, at one time the craft industries (blacksmithing, weaving, wood carving, etc.) were organised on the model of the lineage structure, but in recent times guilds have been created to train apprentices and to regulate the activity of such new craftsmen as the goldsmith, tinker, gun smith, sawyer, carpenter, tailor, barber, builder, leatherworker, shoemaker, and bicycle repairer. These guilds are organised on a contractual basis independent of kinship (Lloyd 1853, pp. 30-44).

In situations of rapid social change, voluntary associations are important as a means of organising people in order to achieve new ends, such as the raising of capital, the regulation of prices, and the provision of extra labour. They are also of great significance to the social scientist in that they reveal cultural values and goals that the participants themselves are unable to formulate. One aspect that has impressed outside observers is the plethora of honorific titles and apparently gratuitous ceremonials. These are found, for example, in Haitian work societies (Metraus 1951, pp. 73-86) and Melanesian cargo cults (Worsley 1957, p. 241), as well as in various African associations (Banton 1957, pp. 181-182). Some writers have seen in such associations a clue to the motivations of the participants and an explanation of the popularity of associations. Discussing some modern urban associations in Nigeria, one anthropologist described "the realism with which this playing at society a La Europeenne is enacted" and stated that "psychologically, it has the significance of a substitute for thrills and achievements which normal life cannot offer" (Nadel 1942, p. 391). Analysing entertainment societies in a Northern Rhodesian town, another writer held that in the 1920s the appeal of this play acting was the vicarious participation in European society, but that by the 1950s the participants' reference group had become the African national elite of professionals and white-collar employees (Mitchell 1956, pp. 12-15). By wearing smart European clothes in a particular style, the members of a dancing group identified themselves with Africans who had advanced further up the modern scale of social status.

Another important aspect of rapid social change is the way new forms of organisation create new roles and relationships. Innovation of this kind is usually a trial and error procedure in which the motivations of the participants are influenced by circumstances they only partly understand. For example, in eastern Nigeria during the middle and late 1940s, numerous associations were developed on the basis of lineage, clan, village, village-group, division and tribe. Their aim was to carry out various economic, educational, political, social and general reforms directly related to changing cultural conditions. Ottenberg (1955) reported that by 1953 almost half the villages of the Afikpo Ibo had such associations. They subscribed loans to help members needing capital for developing trade or farming. They made bicycle paths, improved water supplies, and gave scholarships to promising students. These associations expressed the interests of the young men who, partly because of the war, had learned more about the outside world. These men could not work effectively for modern goals through the traditional institutions, so they formed and supported new associations. The success of voluntary association in the rural villages often reflects increasing consciousness of the outer world. The villagers resent the scorn of outsiders about their backward condition and come together more closely to complete with other villages for new prizes.

Voluntary associations in the cities have many features similar to those in villages, but they differ in that initially they serve only as substitutes for the traditional institutions with which the migrant has lost touch. The first kind of urban association to appear, therefore, is the bereavement benefit society, which takes over the kin group's responsibilities in the event of death. If a member who has no kinfolk within easy reach should die, the society arranges the funeral. If a member has to arrange the funeral of one of his relatives, the society contributes money and attends the ceremonies to support the colleague by honouring his dead. In Abidjan, Ivory, Coast, there is some intermarriage between immigrants from the strongly patrilineal societies of the far interior Savanna zone and women from matrilineal societies of the western coastal zone. Since both parents claim offspring for their own lineages, marital unions are frequently short-lived and often conclude with neither kin group assuming full responsibility for the child. These "lost children" join together in mutual aid societies that play the part of a kin group in helping members learn a trade and in presiding over marriages (Rouch 1963).

It is in the sphere of economic activity that urban associations most evidently create relationships on a new pattern. Among male workers in industrial occupations, the employment situation has forced workers' associations to develop quite rapidly into trade unions. Initially, the workers formed multipurpose societies to meet the whole range of their needs. The first Sudanese trade union, for example, included in its aims mutual help in time of illness, death, and unemployment; the establishment of savings schemes and cooperative societies; and organisation of "Literary and scientific lectures" (Hodgkin 1956, p. 127). The case of the copper mines of Northern Rhocesia in particularly instructive. In the early 1930s, the mine managers introduced a system of tribal representation in order to open channels of worker-management consultation with African employees. It was soon found that in situations of industrial tension, tribal affiliation was rendered irrelevant by the dominant cleavage between employers and mine workers. The Africans' common occupational role was the critical one, and they had to organise on an industrial basis if they were to advance their interests. In the process, they learned new relationships and norms (Epstein 1958). Among non-industrial male workers, such as fishermen, truck drivers, and other self-employed persons, occupational associations tend to remain on a multipurpose level. Women's occupational associations show similar features, although in southern Nigeria there are women's societies that run a bakery, a laundry, a calabash workshop, and a gari mill (Little 1965, p. 127).

The formulation of new roles and relationships is also apparent in the features of voluntary associations that seem to have no useful purpose. As has been mentioned, many of these associations support a much greater variety of ranks and titles than is necessary to the functioning of the organisation. The traditional norms for ascribing social status are in conflict with the new social patterns dictated by the world economy into which the societies are rapidly being propelled.

Voluntary associations, therefore, develop ways of honouring the people they think worthy; the overelaborate system of ranks serves as a means of differentiating the relative merits of members and of giving an indigenous character to values obtained from the new influences. Because members are not always firmly committed to the new ways and treasurers are all too likely to abseond, the associations have to experiment with varying forms of organisation. The proliferation of titled officers provides a justification for involving several members in money matters and other areas important to the society, while the enjoyment of a special title increases the individual member's loyalty. The representation of minor European ceremonials in the conduct of meetings, the use of European languages by some groups, and similar features may be seen as part of a process in which young men brought up in traditional societies based on ascribed status learn instead the principles of conduct important in an achievement oriented society. As one writer has commented: in using English at their meetings, the Africans were learning to handle one of the most important tools of the new culture. When Africans conversed together in English, they showed that they had interests in common which cut across tribal divisions. Furthermore, in the handling of novel concepts they were broadening their intellectual horizons, and making possible closer contact and acquaintance with the world outside. (Epstein 1958, p. 84).

Further support for an interpretation stressing how African urban associations institutionalise new roles and buttress new standards of general conduct may be found in the way associations in a particular town can often be ranked in terms of prestige. At the bottom come the simplest associations, which arrange entertainment for holidays and appeal to the least sophisticated immigrants; the members could not make a success of a more elaborate organisation. Above them come the permanent recreational groups and friendly societies supported by the more ambitious young people. Then come the social clubs of the elite, whose aims are more narrowly defined and whose organisational structure is less complicated. Thus, at the bottom of this scale people are not concerned with innovation; at the top, the new values have been fairly securely established and are supported by other institutions; it is in the middle that the process of adaptation is most in evidence. It should also be mentioned that in emphasising particular standards—whether or not they are now the members of such bodies reinforce processes of social control. In rapidly changing circumstances of social control, problems of delinquency, crime, and dereliction of customary obligations become pressing. Modernist associations reward those people who respond in the approved way and with hold approval from others; in addition to such sanctions, the associations sometimes take direct action against those they see as wrongdoers who are not punished by other institutions. Thus, as several writers have stressed, voluntary associations in African cities have both adaptive and integrative functions (e.g. Banton 1957, Little 1965).

Association as a principle of social grouping is more general, however, than a consideration of friendly societies and clubs might imply. The evidence in Africa makes clear that a variety of new institutions have been obliged by the course of social change to organise on associational lines. The case of trade unions has been touched upon political parties are another instance. They have often developed out of the "welfare societies" and similar bodies organised by the more educated Africans. In the early phases the tendency was toward loose political alliance of the "Congress" type that represented the opposition to colonial rule. With the extension of the franchise, party organisations were needed to marshal supporters, have them registered as electors, explain voting symbols and procedures, spread propaganda, and ascertain public opinion (Hodgkin 1956, pp. 139-168). The organisational basis of parties had to be associational. In most cases, however, majority parties, after independence, have insisted that they serve the widest range of interests and are rebuilding the very structure of society; this has limited the scope for any association that is, or can be represented as, an opposition party.

A similar sequence can be detected in independent religious groups under colonial rule. In the earlier phases of contact, an all-embracing prophetic movement may express the resentments and aspirations of the people, but the independent church later becomes the characteristic institution. The church has a more limited field of action, and the loyalty of its members is maintained by a complex infrastructure of prayer guilds, social clubs, etc. which, like a friendly society, may support members in bereavement. Because their potential members have similar needs and are accustomed to similar social arrangements, trade unions, political parties independent churches, and friendly societies are obliged to organise in similar ways.

It is unusual for research to be designed to investigate the characteristics of associations in pre-literature or developing societies, although frequently the significance of associational activity is revealed in the course of inquiries into other matters. This trend will probably continue. Associations are of interest to the social scientist only if examined from a particular standpoint, which usually entails study of a wider range of institutions. This discussion may have shown some of the merits and limitations of a bird's eye evolutionary approach to the topic and may have indicated that it is more fruitful to study the significance of associations in particular phases of social change. The present need is for the formulation of theories that can be tested cross-culturally; this may result in the substitution of other concepts for them "association" if they will permit the diversity of phenomena to be classified in a manner that relates them more directly to a theory of social organisation.

II

Sociological Aspects

Definitions of the term "voluntary association" as it applies to organisations in modern societies, differ widely, but they generally contain three key elements. A voluntary association is an organised group of persons (1) that is formed in order to further some common interest of its members (2) in which membership is voluntary in the sense that it is neither mandatory nor acquired through birth; and (3) that exist independently of the State. Even this broad definition admits some exceptions. Membership in such voluntary associations as labour unions or professional societies may be a condition of employment or professional practice, and thus may not be truly voluntary. Membership in a church or in a family society may be "inherited" from one's parents and, in that sense, not voluntary. Many voluntary associations are subject to State control to the extent that they must be registered, and agencies of the State often create or sponsor voluntary associations in order to achieve their own ends. (This occurs in both totalitarian and democratic societies: the 4-H Clubs of America, for example, are voluntary associations that direct vocational and other activities for more than two million farm youths, yet they are sponsored by the Extension Service of the US. Department of Agriculture). In spite of the exceptions, however, these three characteristics provide a framework for a consideration of the distinctly sociological importance of voluntary associations.

Defined in these broad terms, voluntary associations include all non state organisations—churches, business firms, labour unions, foundations, private schools and universities, cooperatives, and political parties. In most of the writings on voluntary associations (including the present article), a much narrower definition is used. The broad definition is of great interest historically, however, since it is central to the principle of the freedom of association upon which all voluntary associations depend for their existence. It is also relevant to studies of contemporary associations, since it forces the researcher to play attention to what he is actually studying when he seeks to study the extent of membership in voluntary associations or the functions which voluntary associations serve for their members or for society.

The history of the principle of freedom of association, defined by Laski as "a recognised legal right on the part of all persons to combine for the promotion of purposes in which they are interested" (1931, p. 447), is extremely complex. Briefly, although both guilds (or "gilds") of artisans and corporations existed in antiquity, their existence was defined by the State as a convenience or privilege not as a right (see Corporation Gilds). This tolerance has led to the notion that corporations originated as creatures of the state which is how they are regarded in American legal theory and to the stipulation in some definitions of voluntary associations that they be unincorporated (Mishnun 1934, p. 283). But the distinction is quite meaningless as far as contemporary voluntary associations (at least in the United States) are concerned: whether a voluntary association is incorporated or not is largely a practical question decided by the officers and has few consequences for its activities or its function in society.

There is a fine but clear distinction between the willingness of the state to tolerate the existence of voluntary associations and the right of individuals to create and join associations, provided only that they do not disturb law and order. This right was first won in Europe by guilds and Protestant religious groups; according to Laski (1931, p. 449), in its modern form the right had its origin in Locke's treatment of the churches in his Letter Concerning Toleration. The acceptance by the state of this right is obviously fundamental to the maintenance of civil liberties. It is also central to the most significant role that voluntary associations play in society; since they are created by individuals and are independent of the state, they can serve to mediate between the individual and society (as well as between the individual and such groupings as the professions). Accordingly, the study of voluntary associations can do much to illuminate what is probably the most general problem in all the social sciences; the relationship of the individual, with his needs, to society, with its requirements.

Although all non state, common purpose organisations with voluntary memberships are voluntary associations, that is, organisations whose existence is dependent upon freedom of association, the present article will focus upon organisations that meet both of two additional criteria. First, the major activity of the organisation is not related to the business of making a living, that is, to the economic activities of its members (as in the case of professional associations, trade unions, or cooperatives). Second, the volunteer (i.e. nonsalaried) members constitute a majority of the participants (as they do not in corporations, universities, or foundations, in which the directors or trustees are in a minority vis-a-vis the employees, faculty, or students), "Spare-time, participatory associations" might be the best description of the associations most frequently referred to in this article.

Voluntary associations that do not meet these criteria are described in detail elsewhere in the encyclopaedia, "Making-a-living" associations include business firms (see Business Management: Corporation: Industry; Small, trade associations (See Cartels and Trade Associations), production, marketing, and consumer cooperatives (see Cooperatives), professional associations (see Professions) and labour unions (See Labour Unions) "Minority membership" associations include philanthropic foundations (See Foundation; Philanthorophy), private schools and universities (See

Educations' Universities) and lobbies (See Interest Groups; Lobbeying). These organisations have many of the characteristics of spare time participatory associations, but they are sufficiently different in their internal characteristics and in the functions they serve, both for their members and for society, to warrant separate discussion.

Churches and political parties are voluntary associations that also are not discussed in detail in this article, on the grounds that the research literature upon which the article is based generally does not include them and that they are discussed in detail elsewhere in the encyclopaedia (See Parties, Political Clubs; Religious Organisation; Sects and Cults). The rationale for excluding them in rather weak, however, since they are spare time participatory organisations that are independent of the state. Both Fig is (1913) and Lindsay (1943) based their distinctions between the state and society upon the assumption that both churches and political parties are voluntary associations.

The plan of this article is as follows. First come a brief review of the research evidence on the distribution of voluntary associations in modern societies and on the extent of participation in them. This is followed by a description of some of the classifications that sociologists have developed in order to construct typologies of voluntary associations. Then comes a discussion of the organisational processes that are most characteristic of voluntary associations. Finally, there is a summary of the major assertions that have been made about the functions which voluntary associations serve for individuals and for society, together with some discussion of the evidence that either exists or is needed to demonstrate that these functions are in fact performed.

Extent and Membership

The data on the number of spare time, participatory voluntary associations (hereafter called voluntary associations) in modern societies and on the proportion of the population that belongs to them are scattered, and comparisons between studies are made difficult by differences in definitions and in research objectives. What is badly needed—and what has not as yet even been approximated—is a definition of a voluntary association that can be applied cross culturally and that would permit a count of the number of voluntary associations which exist in various societies and in a sample of communities within societies. Such a count should be reported both as a total and on a per capita basis. Membership in different kinds of voluntary associations should be determined by sample surveys, and the extent of membership participation should be ascertained by studies of the organisations themselves. Finally, measures should be obtained of the importance of this activity to the life of the society.

In the absence of these ideal data, something can be learned from an examination of the handful of studies that do exist.

These studies have found voluntary associations to be characteristic of urban societies and the most urbanised areas of all societies. Why is this so? Population density is certainly a major reason; the more people there are in a community, the more forms of interaction of all Kinds exist. The higher socioeconomic status of urban residents is another explanation; urban residents belong to voluntary associations not only because they are urbanities but also because they tend to be educated, socially active people. In a classic essay, Louis Wirth cited the weakness of kinship, family, and neighbourhood ties in the city as an explanation: "Being reduced to a stage of virtual importance as an individual, the urbanite is bound to exert himself by joining with others of similar interests into organised groups to obtain his ends" (1938, p.22).

Even sharper differences than rural-urban ones are found between different rural societies. Rural Japanese communities, for example, have many voluntary associations (Norbeck 1962), while towns in southern Italy have none or very few (Banfield 1958). A possible explanation, based on studies of rural Denmark (Anderson and Anderson 1958) and West Africa (Little 1965), is that voluntary associations are both numerous and influential in rural communities undergoing rapid urbanisation.

Since Tocqueville made his famous observation in Democracy in America— "In no country of the world has the principle of association been more successfully used or applied to a greater multitude of objects than in America" (1835, 1945, Vol. I, p. 198)—and Bryce made his in The American Commonwealth— "They are created, extended, and worked in the United States more quickly and effectively than in any other country" (1888, 1933, Vol. 2, pp. 281-282) the United States has often been described by observers as "a nation of joiners", Max Weber also expressed this opinion: "What is, in qualitative terms, the association-land par excellence? Without doubt America..." (1911, p. 53). It is not clear whether he was influenced by Tocqueville or Bryce, or by his own observations on his visit to the United States in 1905.

In spite of the number of such remarks in the literature of commentary upon American society, and without denying the central importance of voluntary associations in American life, it should be noted that perhaps too much emphasis has been placed upon the scope and uniqueness of the American pattern. The research of Warner and his associates (Warner and Lunt 1941) uncovered 357 associations in Yankee City (pop. 17,000), and Bushee (1945) found 245 associations in Boulder, Colorado (pop. 12,000); but Max Weber (1911) found some three hundred associations in a German city of 30,000 merely by consulting the city directory. The observation is frequently made that voluntary associations are most common in America and the Protestant countries of Europe, and indeed the contrast between the Protestant countries and the Roman Catholic countries is quite marked; but the prevalence of voluntary associations in such different countries as Japan (Norbeck 1962), Nigeria (Little 1965), Ghana (Wallerstein 1964), Thailand (Riggs 1962a), and Israel (Eisenstadt 1956) indicates that the pattern is by no means confined to Protestant countries. The research evidence is scattered, and contradictory claims are common. In France, for example, Rose found that voluntary associations are both few in number and of limited influence (1954b, pp. 50—115), while Gallagher found over three hundred associations in a provincial town of 50,000 (1957).

Only in America has sufficient research been undertaken to provide a reasonably accurate picture of the extent of participation in voluntary associations. Alfred O. Hero has summarised much of this research, as follows:

The proportion of the population affiliated with organisations varied considerably with the type of community. For example... (a National Opinion Research Center) study of Denver (Colorado) in 1949 reported that 64 per cent said they belonged either to voluntary organisations or to labour unions. Elimination of those who were members of unions probably would have lowered the figure to around 50-55 per cent. Morris Axelrod (1956, pp. 13—18) reported that 37 per cent of Detroit (Michigan) adults were affiliated with neither voluntary associations nor labour unions, that half of the 63 per cent who were affiliated were members of only one, and that a large number of those with only one affiliation were members of unions... When trade unions, religious bodies, and parent teacher associations were excepted, Basil G. Zimmer and Amos H. Hawley (1959, p. 198) reported that only 43 per cent of adults in Flint, Michigan, and 25 per cent in its suburbs and urban fringe areas were affiliated with organisations. Percentages of adults unaffiliated with organisations (typically including trade unions) reported in other locales have been as follows: Bennington (Vermont 35 per cent (Scott 1957, pp. 315—326) Chicago 35 per cent (Goldhamer 1942, p. 20) Muncie Indiana 42 per cent (Lynd and Lynd 1929, p. 308) Boulder (Colorado) 48 per cent ... Bushee 1945, p.218); a rural-urban fringe in Oregon 49 per cent (Martin 1952, p. 689); a small city and environs in Ohio 50 per cent (Lazarsfeld et. al. 1944 p. 173); among employed adults in New York City 52 per cent... (Komarovsky 1946, pp. 689-690), Newburyport (Massachusetts)—59 per cent (Warner and Lunt 1941, p. 329 Westchester (county in New York) 60 per cent ... (Lundberg et al. 1934, pp. 129, 136); and among Mary leaders ages 16-25-74 per cent... (Bell 1938, p. 168), (1960, pp. 115-116).

The summary has been presented in full in order to demonstrate the difficulties of obtaining comparable data on this topic; in fact, the noncomparability of the data probably accounts for more of the variation from study to study than do the differences in date, location, or type of community. This non-comparability stems in part from variations in the definition of a voluntary association that is explicitly or implicitly used, and in part from the household interview method used in these studies. Respondents may both fail to recall and seek to impress; thus, interview data underestimate the proportion of American adults who are at least inactive members in associations (which is probably over 75 per cent) and overestimate the proportion who are active members (which is probably somewhat less than 20 per cent). Although this is only an informed guess, it is not without empirical foundation. Babchuk and Edwards, for example, reported that the "Detroit area study" found that 63 per cent of the adult population belonged to voluntary associations, but that of these only 28 per cent had contributed any time to an association in the previous three months (1965, pp. 150-151).

Membership in American voluntary associations (and presumably in those in other industrialised countries as well) is not random; some segments of the population are much more likely to participate than are others. Whites are more likely to participate than are Negroes, Jews more likely than Protestants, and Protestants more likely than Roman Catholics; urban and rural nonfarm residents more likely than farm residents; parents more likely that non parents; frequent voters more likely than non voters. The largest and most consistent differences in participation are those in socio-economic status, whether measured by income, occupation, homeownership, or educational level. A majority of Americans of higher status belong to voluntary associations, and a majority of people of lower status do not (Wright and Hyman 1958, Hausknechi 1962).

Explanations for these patterns of differential membership are not hard to find. Membership in a voluntary association is a form of social interaction, and people who are deprived of a broad range of social interaction (farmers, Negroes, immigrant Roman Catholics, widows) are almost by definition less likely to belong to voluntary associations. More difficult to explain are variations that appear to exist—both in the number of associations and in the proportion of the population that participates—from one society to another. A number of plausible hypotheses have been advanced; they derived from the functions which voluntary associations seem to serve for the individual, for subgroups in society, and for the society as a whole, and they are reviewed in later sections of this article.

Classification into Types

Although it is necessary to discuss spare-time, participatory voluntary associations as a generic type, it must not be assumed that the thousands of such associations which exist in a society are all of one type. On the contrary, the range of variation is probably greater than that which exists among government and business organisations.

A variety of typologies has been developed, each useful for a particular purpose. For many purposes a simple classification based upon the stated program or the manifest purpose of the association is sufficient. Hausknecht, for example, in a further analysis of the American data used by Wright and Hyman (1958), developed the eight classifications show in Table 1.

Table - 1. Distribution of Voluntary Association Members by Type of Association

Type of Association	*Percent belonging*
Civic and Service	38
Lodges and fraternal	31
Church and religious	25
Social and recreational	16
Veternas, military, patriotic	14
Economic, occupational, professional	9
Cultural, educational, alumni	4
Political and pressure	4
Total	(853)*

Source: Adopted from Hausknecht 1962, p. 84.

* Percentages add to more than 100, since some individuals belong to more than one type of association.

Although the typology in Tabel 1 gives a broad picture of the patterns of membership, it provides no information about the structure of the associations or the latent functions that they perform; in fact, little is told even about their manifest functions, since there is a great deal of overlap in their activities. Community service activities, for example, are a major part of the program not only of civic associations but also of lodges, church organisations, and veterans' groups.

Other classifications which utilize either structure of function as a variable have been developed. Sherwood Fox (1953), for example, examined the functions performed by some five thousand associations and based a classification upon the distinction between majoral, minoral, and medial organisations. Majoral associations are those which serve the interests of the major institutions of society: business, professional, scientific, educational, labour, and agricultural associations. Minoral associations serve the interests of significant minorities in the population: women's clubs, church organisations, hobby clubs, and, above all, ethnic associations. Medial associations mediate between major segments or institutions in the society. For example, parent teacher associations mediate between the family and the school system; social welfare organisations mediate between those who provide financial or other aid and the underprivileged population; veterans' groups mediate between war veterans and the government; and voluntary health associations mediate between scientists and the public, as well as between individuals suffering from a particular disease and the medical profession.

A structural distinction, that between "corporate type" and "federation type" organisations, was developed by Sills (1957) to analyse problems of organisational structure and control in national organisations. This distinction has many parallels. Some national states are loose federations of semi-autonomous component units, while others are highly centralised (see *Centralisation and Decentralisation*), Churches may also be classified in a similar way. At one extreme are "congregational" churches, in which each parish is responsible for its own affairs; at the other extreme are "episcopal" churches, in which ultimate authority resides in the parent organisation (see *Religious Organisation*).

A typology of voluntary associations based upon a structural variable ("accessibility", or who is eligible for membership) and two functional variables ("status-conferring capacity", or the extent to which membership bestows prestige, and "instrumental expressive", or whether activities are directed toward the behaviour of non-members or of members) has been developed by Babchuk and Gordon (1962, p. 38). "Instrumental" associations are generally termed "interest groups" by political scientists (see *Interest Groups*).

Organisational Processes

Since voluntary associations are a type of formal organisation, they exhibit some of the same social processes and social pathologies as do other organisations. The present article will focus upon four processes that are of fundamental importance to an understanding of voluntary associations: institutionalisation, minority rule, goal displacement, and goal succession.

Institutionalisation: In its broadest meaning, institutionalization is the process through which patterns of behaviour and expectations of behaviour on the part of others become established. Marriage, the market place, and the burying of the dead are all examples of institutions. One feature of an institution in this sense is that it is unplanned: only after it has been established is a pattern termed an institution. As Walton H. Hamilton said of the institution we call feudalism:

The feudal regime was an empirical sort of an affair, men of iron lorded it over underlings as they could, yielded to their betters as they were compelled and maintained such law and order as the times allowed: but with its passing its sprawling arrangements and befuddled functions were turned into office and estate ordained of God (1932, p. 87).

As it applies to organisations, institutionalisation means the unplanned process that turns a loosely organised group of adherents to an idea or a goal into a formal organisation (see *Social Institutions*, Article on *The Concept*). Since it is a social process, institutionalisation may be studied at any point on the time continuum that runs from the emergence of an idea to the death of an organisation through strangulation by its own rules of procedure. John E. Tsouderos, for example, has studied what he called the formalisation process in established organisations. He selected ten voluntary associations and applied time series analysis to five quantitative variables: number of members, total annual income, total annual expenditures, values of organisational property, and number of administrative employees. This analysis revealed two cycles in the history of the associations: a "cycle of growth" and a "cycle of formalisation". Membership started to decline at the point that separated these two cycles, annual income started to decline midway in the cycle of formalisation, and the other three variables increased slowly through both cycles. As used by

Tsouderos, "institutionalisation" means essentially "bureaucratisation" (See Tsouderos 1955; Chapin and Tsouderos 1956; see also *Organisations*, article on *Theories of Organisations*).

Institutionalization may also be studied by examining the processes through which voluntary associations become established as the institutional expressions of social movements, Wendell King (1956), for example, has identified three phases in the "life cycle" of social movements: the incipient phase, in which a handful of believers works toward a goal established by the founder (often a charismatic leader); the organisational phase, in which voluntary associations are established; and the stable phase, in which the voluntary associations (if they survive) become increasingly professionalised, bureaucratic, and conservative (see Charisma; Social Movements).

In spite of analyses such as those of Tsouderos and King, systematic study of the institutionalisation process has hardly begun. Much of the interest in the impact of institutionalisation and formalisation centres on the transformation of organisational goals over time (see "Goal succession", below). What is badly needed is historical research that is guided by organisational theory. A beginning has been made in such research as Sheldon Messinger's study of the growth and decline of the Townsend Movement, a depression born scheme to restore prosperity in the United States by the Government's making monthly payments to the aged (1955); Gusfield's study of the history of the Woman's Christian Temperance Union (1955; 1957); and Zald and Denton's study of the transformation of the YMCA from evangelism to general service (1963). Awaiting similar historical analysis are such organisations as the Sons of Liberty and the Committees of Correspondence, two voluntary associations in the early history of the United States that were dissolved when the anti-British purposes for which they were established were achived through the American Revolution and the establishment of the Continental Congress; the American Anti-Slavery Society, which split through internal dissension and controversy over policy matters some twenty years before the Emancipation Proclamation and the Indian National Congress, which after India achieved independence became the increasingly conservative Congress party.

A third use of the concept of institutionalisation regards it not necessarily as a process that develops over time but, rather, as a characteristic that distinguishes between voluntary associations at one point in time. Some voluntary associations have goals and programs that are oriented towards the gradual improvement of the existing order. Their members therefore bring a relatively low degree of affect to their participation, and the organisational structure is relatively formal and matter of fact. Such highly institutionalised organisations may be called formal organisation-like associations. Other voluntary associations have goals and programs that are much more radical and ideological, and are more at variance with what the participants believe to be the norms of society; their members bring a relatively high degree of affect to their participation, and the organisational structure is likely to be informal and fluid. These less institutionalised organisations may be called social movement—like associations. Figure 1 presents a two dimensional scheme for classifying voluntary associations; institutionalisation in the sense of "formal organisation like" is one of the dimensions, and the lay-versus-professional base of the membership is the other. Since the associations given as examples in Figure 1 were selected rather arbitrarily and for illustrative purposes, there is no attempt to show that there is an absence of correlation between the two dimensions. What is apparent is that a membership base of professionals does not necessarily result in a formal organisation like association, although examples in the upper left hand quadrant of the figure are relatively hard to find. The scheme shown in Figure 1 is given not as a definite finding of research but, rather as a heuristic device to demonstrate the potentialities of typologies for generating research hypotheses.

Minority rule: Since voluntary associations can exist only in societies in which freedom of association exists, and since such societies are more or less democratic in their ethos and political structure, there is an expectation that members will taken an active part in the affairs of the association and that democratic procedures will govern its conduct. This expectation often is not met; although most voluntary associations have constitutions, bylaws, or oral traditions that call for full participation by the members, the "iron law of oligarchy" formulated by Robert Michels generally has greater weight:

Organisation implies the tendency to oligarchy. In every organisation, whether it be a political party, a professional union, or any other association of the kind, the aristocratic tendency manifests itself very clearly. The mechanism of the organisation, while conferring a solidarity of structure, induces serious changes in the organised mass, completely inverting the respective position of the leaders' and the led. As a result of organisation, every party or professional union becomes divided into a minority of directors and a majority of directed (1911, 1959, p. 32).

Figure-1

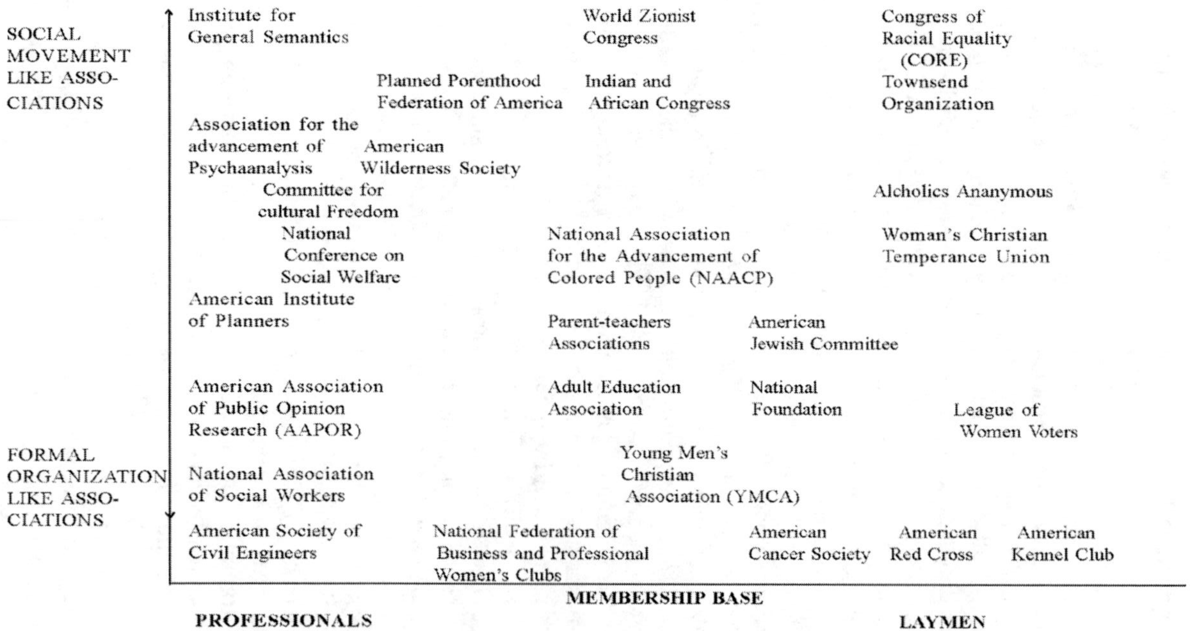

Figure- 1 A Two Dimensional Scheme for Classifying Voluntary Associations.

Michels was not the first social scientist to comment upon the oligarchic nature of voluntary associations; in fact, by what presumably is merely an interesting coincidence, in the year that Michels' Political Parties was published, Max Weber made a very similar observation:

In every organisation, whether it be called a party, a society, a club, or whatever, authority in effect always takes the form of minority rule—sometimes the dictatorship of an individual. It is the rule of one or more persons who are qualified by a process of selection or by virtue of their competence to assume the tasks of leadership and who have *de facto* authority in the organisation. (1911, p. 56).

It was perhaps Michels' good fortune in adapting Ricardo's striking phrase "the iron law of wages" to his purposes that has made his analysis better known than Weber's. Neither carried his analysis of the determinants of minority rule very far. In a crucial phrase, Michels said it came about "as a result of organisation" and Weber wrote of the dominance of "professional personnel". (See the biography of Michels).

Critics of minority rule in voluntary associations have often invoked "membership apathy" as an explanation for it. Barber (1950) however, has pointed out that these critics offer no evidence for the existence of apathy as a psychological trait; rather, the sociologist can demonstrate that the social structure of role obligations and the structural needs of the organisations themselves together militate against "complete" participation. Many other social scientists have contributed observations and research findings toward an understanding of the related phenomena of membership inactivity and minority rule; Table 2 summarizes much of this literature.

Table - 2. Some Determinants of Membership Inactivity and Minority Rule in Voluntary Associations

Locus of the determinant	Illustrative citations
Organisational Structure	
Representative Government	Barber 1950, pp. 490-91
Large number of members	Michels (1911). 1959, p. 26
	Truman 1951, p. 141
	Tsouderos, 1955, p. 209
Functional Specialisation	Barber 1950, pp. 490-91
	Michels (1911), 1959, p. 400
Membership heterogeneity and	Bendix 1947, p. 494
Absence of consensus	Selznick 1952, p. 308
	Simon 1947, p. 114

Institutionalisation and formalisation	Starbuck 1965, pp. 477—480 Tsouderos 1955, p. 209 Weber 1911
Leadership requirements sepcialised skills	Barber 1950, pp. 490-91
Availability of time	Barber 1950, pp. 492-93 Garceau 1941, p. 54
Temperoment	Riesman and Glazer 1950 Selznick 1943, p. 52
Organisational activities	
Absence of concrete tasks	Sills 1957, pp. 36—42
Conflicts with other interests;	Barber 1950, p. 486
Segmental participation	Selznick 1952, pp. 286—288 Truman 1951, pp. 157—167
Disparity between reasons for Joining and organisational activities	Cartwright 1951 Lewin 1948 Rose 1954b, p. 64.

The array of determinants listed in Table 2 is very similar to the array that might be developed to demonstrate the impossibility of the full participation of all citizens in any democracy. Since it is impossible for all citizens to play active roles, governments are established; through the process of elections, representatives are selected who are empowered to speak for their constituencies. In many democracies, however, full participation in even the basic activity of voting for representatives is not even approximated. Voluntary associations should be different from national societies, it is often claimed, since their members join of their own free will, and in many instances they do have higher participation rates than national states. But similar social structural determinants serve to depress full participation.

Goal displacement: Since voluntary associations like all organisations—are established for the purpose of realising some short-term or long-term goal, the study of the relationship of these goals to other aspects of an organisation's existence has occupied the attention of many researchers. How goals are established, how decisions are made concerning what activities will serve to realise a goal, how goals are interpreted to the community—these and many other questions are implicit or explicit in research on voluntary associations (see Organisations, Article on Organisational Goals).

The fact that an organisation's charter or statement of purpose contains an explicit description of the goals it is to pursue is no guarantee that the organisation's procedures will be single mindedly directed toward these ends. In fact, it is the procedures themselves that often serve to deflect the organisation from its goals:

The generic problem of goal preservation may be stated as follows: In order to accomplish their goals, organisations establish a set of procedures or means. In the course of following these procedures, however the subordinates or members to whom authority and functions have been delegated often come to regard them as ends in themselves, rather than as means toward the achievement of organisational goals. As a result of this process, the actual activities of the organisation become contended around the proper functioning of organisation procedures, rather than upon the achievement of the initial goals. (Sills 1957, p. 62).

The analysis of the phenomenon called goal displacement has occupied the attention of many sociologists—from Michels and Weber to Blau, Gouldner, Lipset, Merton, and Selznick; a summary of this research tradition is given elsewhere (Sills 1957, pp. 62—77) and need not be repeated in detail here. One source of goal displacement is the desire of active participants to retain high status positions in the organisation; in order to do this, they tend to focus their activities upon self-serving rather than goal-directed activities. Perhaps the most striking example is that of leaders of labour unions, who are understandably reluctant to forfeit their status and income in order to "go back to the bench".

A second source of goal displacement lies in the strict enforcement of organisational rules and the slavish carrying out of organizational procedures. The sentiments that are developed to buttress the rules and perform the procedures often become more intense than is technically necessary; following the rules and carrying out the procedures become ends in themselves.

The informal structures that develop within organisations are a third source of goal displacement. Hundreds of studies, starting with the famous research at the Hawthorne Works of the Western Electric Company in Chicago in the years 1927 to 1932 (Roethlisberger and Dickson 1939), have demonstrated that informally created groups within organisations are not only crucial to goal achievement but are also for example, through the informal establishment of production norms that are lower than those desired by management responsible for a certain amount of goal displacement. (See *Groups*, article on *The Study of Groups, Industrial Relations*, article on *Human Relations*).

Goal succession: The literature on the two major pathologies of voluntary associations, the tendency toward obligarchy and the displacement of goals, leads to fundamentally pessimistic conclusions. In spite of the best of intentions, these writers say, the inherent nature of the process of organisation is such that minorities will gain control in order to serve their own ends; as a result, the purposes for which the organisation is established will be blunted. The two major landmarks in this literature illustrate the point. Michels' Political Parties (1911) concludes that the prospects for democracy in social democratic parties and labour unions are dim. Selznick's TVA and the Grass Roots (1949) concludes that the TVA'S delegation of certain phases of its agricultural program to local organisations led to these organisations' being "co-opted" into the policy-making apparatus of the TVA itself, which in turn caused the TVA to be deflected from some of its major goals.

These pessimistic conclusions have not gone unchallenged. For instance, Bendix has pointed out that if the supposed iron law of oligarchy is to prevail in an organisation, there must be dissensus among its members:

It is misleading to assume that a ruling elique can deliberately prevent the "success" of an organisation, while everybody else agrees on the methods and desirability of achieving it. Rather, an organized minority can maintain its power and it can make its idea of success prevail, as long as disagreement is widespread both with regard to the meaning of "success" and to the methods by which it is to be achieved (1947, p. 494).

And Lipset, while concluding on the basis of his study of a "deviant case" (a democratically controlled labour union) that "the functional requirements for democracy cannot be met most of the time in most unions" (1954, p. 121), also concluded that democracy is not a functional prerequisite of effectiveness. "Even the most dictatorial union is a better protector of workers' economic interests and of political democracy within the larger society than no union, provided that the union is not a tool either of the state or of the employer" (ibid., p. 122).

The recurrent theme in the vast commentary upon the "iron law of oligarchy" is that the law holds true only under certain circumstances, and even when it does hold true, other democratic values may nevertheless be furthered. In a frontal attack upon those who see only tragedy in the processes of organization, Gouldner asserted that "there is every reason to assume that the underlying tendencies which are likely to inhibit the democratic process' are just as likely to impair authoritarian rule. There cannot be an iron law of oligarchy unless there is an iron law of democracy" (1955, 1961, p. 80). Similarly, the literature of criticism of the concept of goal displacement admits the existence of the pathology but points out that the new goals may be an improvement upon the old ones.

Peter Blau's study of bureaucracy in two government agencies is the first landmark in this revisionist literature. He observed that the agencies did not necessarily behave in a rigid, "bureaucratic" way when their goals were achieved or made irrelevant by events; rather, they shifted toward new goals. Blau called this process the "succession of goal", and described it as follows:

The attainment of organisational objectives generates a strain toward finding new objectives. To provide incentives for its members and to justify its existence, an organization has to adopt new goals as its old ones are realized (1955, p. 243 in the 1964 edition).

The attainment of an organisation's objectives in any clear cut sense is a relatively rare event, consequently, there have been few studies of the consequences of success for an organisation. An exception is Sills' study of the National Foundation for Infantile Paralysis, carried out on the eve of the elimination of infantile paralysis as a threatening disease because of the development of the Salk vaccine. His conclusion, that "the Foundation will in the future make a successful adjustment to the achievement of its major goal... (because) the organisation has in fact already been transformed in large part by its Volunteers, into something other than a special purpose association" (1957, p. 270) has been borne out by events. In 1967 the foundation was still a successful voluntary health association, concentrating upon research into and treatment of birth defects.

More commonly although there have been very few studies of such situations—an organisations's environment changes in such a way as to make its goals irrelevant or unobtainable. Table 3 summarizes the relevant findings of studies of four organisations that have had to cope with such changes; two unsuccessful organisations (the Woman's Christian Temperance Union and the Townsend Organisation) and two successful organizations (the YMCA and the American National Red Cross). Since these data are fragmentary and subject to all the limitations the apply to the case study method, they cannot be used as a basis for specifying the conditions under which voluntary associations do and do not adjust to environmental conditions. What they do suggest, however, is the value of comparative research into organisational goal succession.

Functions for Individuals and Society

The functions that voluntary associations are said to perform for individuals and for society may be broadly classified into two groups; manifest (those which are intended and recognized by the participants) and latent (those which are neither intended nor recognized by the participants, but can be observed by the social scientist). Both types of

Table-3 Selected Aspects of the Organizational adaptation of four Voluntary associations*

	UNSUCCESSFUL ORGANIZATIONS		SUCCESSFUL ORGANIZATIONS	
Initial goal	Woman's Christian Temperance Union Encourage abstinence, Particularly among lowerclass people	Townsend organization National Pensions for the aged to alleviate economic dislocation	Young Men's Chistian Association improve the spiritual mental, and social condition of young men	American National Red Cross Mitigale Suffering during wars and other calamities
Additional or Secondary goal	Improve the Welfare of lower Class people	None	Physical education	Serve as chartered agency of the government, directing voluntary aid to sick and wounded during time of war
Characteristics of original membership	Upper-middle and middle class women	Mostly elderly Men and women	Lay leadership Middle-class protestant membership of young men	Largely upper and upper-middle-class men and women
Environmental changes requiring adaptation	Increased permissiveness of drinking norms in middle class groups	End of the depression private pension plans	Secularization of society Emergence of new concepts concerning personality development and character development	End of World War I and World War II Organizational structure and financing too great for disaster relief only Increased governmental disaster relief

Table-3 *Contd...*

	UNSUCCESSFUL ORGANIZATIONS		SUCCESSFUL ORGANIZATIONS	
New or added goals	Express moral indignation Censure the new middle class	provide recreation for the aged Maintain the organization by retail sales	Increased emphasis up on social and othletic activities less emphasis upon evangelical activities	Public health activities Blood donor Program
Consequences for the Organization	Lower-middle and lower-class membership No change in size "An organization in retreal".	End of effective recruiting sharp decline in membership	Membership broadened to include boys, women, non-protestants Professional leadership Emphasis upon Buildings	Increased size and influence More successful preacetime fund raising*

* *An analysis of these four associations may be found in Sills 1957, pp. 258—264.*

Sources: Woman's christian Temparance Union, Gusfield 1955, Townsend Organization Messinger, 1955, Young Men's Christian Association, Pence 1939, Zald & Denton 1963, American National Red Cross Dulles, 1950.

functions are important, and each presents problems of verification; by far the most challenging problems are those presented by latent functions (see *Functional Analysis,* article on *Varieties of Functional Analysis*).

The literature on voluntary associations is filled with assertions about the latent functions that they perform. How may such assertions be verified? Ideally, comparable situations should be studied in which a given kind of voluntary association is and is not present. If the observed function were to be performed in the former situation but not in the latter, then there would be a presumption that the voluntary association was the crucial element is the situation. The difficulties involved in verification of type are enormous, since it is seldom possible to approach the conditions of a controlled experiment, that is, to assign populations to the two situations at random and to hold other factors constant. (Social processes that occur within voluntary associations may be studied by field or laboratory experiments; see Weick 1965; Zelditch and Hopkins 1961, See also *Experimental Design: Groups; Sociometry*). For this reason, latent functions must be accepted largely on the basis of their "logical" character—that is, though "mental experimentation" and on the basis of the absence of any conflicting evidence. Historical analysis is another method of overcoming the difficulties of creating experimental designs; that is, methods of establishing causal relations that are adequate for a historical explanation are, logically, adequate for a functional explanation. The criteria for accepting historical explanations as adequate, however, are much in dispute (For an example of the value of historical research for the study of voluntary associations, see Lipset 1950; for the views of two historians, see *Historiography,* article on *The Rhetoric of History; History,* article on *Social History.* So-called field studies or case studies, with all of their limitations (see Scott 1965), are by far the most common method of research into voluntary associations, and most of the functions described in this article are based upon field observations tested in varying degrees by comparative analysis (See Udy 1965 for discussion of the usefulness of the comparative method in the study of organizations).

(1) Functions for Individuals: The notion that individuals seek out and join a voluntary association in order to find an outlet for an interest is over simplified, since there is considerable evidence that most individuals join an association only after they are urged or invited to do so. (See, for example, Sills 1957, pp. 78—115). Nevertheless, after they become members, it may be presumed that individuals benefit to some extent from the organisations's program, whether it be the satisfactions of sociability, recreation, service, or political action. Manifest functions of this kind, important as they are, require no explanation here. Rather, attention will be given to two latent functions of participation; social integration and training in organisational skills.

In assessing the findings that are reported, it must be remembered that much of the evidence has been obtained from participants rather than from both participants and non-participants.

The researcher is faced with the same problem of self-selection that plagues students of communication: since people expose themselves to televised speeches and newspaper and magazine articles (to say nothing of church sermons) with which they are already in basic agreement, it is often difficult to detect changes in opinion through audience research. Similarly, the minority in a society that is active in voluntary associations tends to be self-selected in ways that minimize the chances of the activity's having a measurable impact upon them. This problem is, of course, compounded by the difficulty of measuring changes in individuals and isolating the influences that brought them about.

Social integration: That people interact with other when they participate in a voluntary association is rather obvious, and it may be assumed that the benefits of interaction—easing loneliness, learning norms, acquiring information are among the most frequent functions of membership for the individuals involved. What is more problematic is whether to use Cooley's terms—secondary groups such as voluntary associations serve the same integrative functions as primary groups. Wirth (1938, p. 20) and many others have expressed the view that the weakness of family and neighbourhood ties in modern (or urban) society is compensated for by participation involuntary associations, but such statements do not constitute proof.

The research evidence from studies of American society is inconclusive (see for example, Babchuk and Edwards 1965, in which material on many kinds of associations is reviewed). There is no doubt that some people achieve family like satisfactions from participation; this is most true of lodges, fraternal orders, and such self-help associations as Alcoholics Anonymous. In most other associations, however, the segmental, part-time, and task oriented nature of the activity precludes the development of true primary group ties. What is much more likely is that people who have satisfactory primary-group ties are more likely to join voluntary associations a reversal of the direction of causality implied by the integration hypothesis. There is considerable evidence that this is so;

for example, Jacoby (1965, p. 166) found that persons with primary-group ties (that is, persons who are living with others) are more likely to join expressive associations than are persons living alone.

One explanation for the absence of evidence of integrative functions in the United States is that it is relatively society, in which the family and the neighbourhood continue to fulfil their historic functions. Janowitz (1952) for example has explicitly challenged Wirth's assertions about the anonymity of urban life by describing how the residents of Chicago (the nation's second largest city, and same city that Wirth studied) are bound to family and neighbourhood groups. In another statement in this continuing debate, Kornhauser pointed out that the evidence of the survival of primary groups in a mass society is not in itself very significant; the groups may persist, but their functions may be considerably weakened. For example, primary group ties may be more easily broken because they receive less support from the institutional structure of society (see *Mass Society*).

The extent to which voluntary associations serve social integrative functions in industrial societies has not as yet been satisfactorily measured. Much the same can be said for this role of voluntary associations in the developing countries, although there are grounds for assuming that voluntary associations are more important in this respect in societies that are in a stage of rapid detribalization and urbanization. Wallerstein, for example, noted that throughout tropical Africa in the post-colonial era "new voluntary associations sprang up to perform the services that the tribe, the family, and the government could not perform" (1964, p. 320).

Training in organisational skills: The social skills necessary for an individual to function effectively in an organisation—serving as a committee member, writing minutes and reports, following Robert's Rules of Order—are learned not at all in the family setting and only imperfectly in the school system. Yet it is precisely these skills that a democracy requires of large numbers of people if positions of power are to be rotated. Inspection of the campaign literature circulated by candidates for posts ranging from village trustee to senator reveals the importance placed by the candidates upon the associations of which they are members. Although candidates list these affiliations to demonstrate their dedication to the community welfare, the lists also serve as certificates of organisational skill. Consider, for example, the city of Lincoln, Nebraska (pop. 150,000), described by Babchuk and Edwards (1965, p.160). After intensive study they concluded that there were over two thousand voluntary associations in that city that met regularly during the year. Since each association had at least one officer, and many had several plus a committee structure of some kind, the total number of residents who received some training in organisational skills in the course of a year is impressive. Here is an example of the reverse of what economists call economies of scale; the more fragmented the organisational structure is, the more individuals are trained.

In societies that are undergoing the transition from tribalism to modernism, the impact of such training is even more dramatic.

As Wallerstein (1964) has described in detail, the voluntary associations in tropical Africa that the colonial powers had encouraged as a means of spreading modern values became in the end effective instruments of liberation: the presidents of debating societies and football associations became through these experiences trained leaders of anticolonial movements.

(2) Functions for Society: There is necessarily some overlap between functions that voluntary associations perform for individuals and those that they perform for society. For example, the training of individuals in organisational skills not only provides satisfactions for them and enables them to advance their careers; it also provides the total society with fresh cadres of leaders who have new perspectives on problems, thereby stimulating social change. The distinction is an important one analytically, however, since a function that may benefit individuals (e.g. through opportunities for self-expression) may be detrimental to society (e.g. if self-expression takes the form of violence). Even in the more frequent instances of functions being beneficial for both individuals and society, this distinction is necessary (see *Functional* analysis, article on *Structural-Functional Analysis*).

Since the range of organisations encompassed by the term "voluntary association" is so broad, some rather stringent limits must be placed upon a discussion of the functions of voluntary associations for society. Even with self-imposed limitations the task is formidable, which perhaps explains the absence of any synthetic discussion of the topic in the sociological literature. Most writers on voluntary associations have devoted a few sentences or paragraphs to the topic, no one has provided an extensive treatment.

The discussion in this section focuses upon six functions that voluntary associations are said to serve for society. As in the case of functions for individuals, the evidence the at these functions are actually performed is uneven, and the problems of verification are largely unsolved. It is noteworthy that the functions described are all positive; few students of voluntary associations have pointed out any dysfunctions. An exception to this generalization is the effect that voluntary associations have on social mobility; although most American researchers have concluded that voluntary associations either provide avenues for upward social mobility or at least confirm prestige earned in other ways, a number of British studies have indicated that the class based membership of many voluntary associations erects barriers to upward social mobility (Morris 1965, p. 200).

Mediation: The term "secondary groups", as it applies to voluntary associations, indicates that associations mediate between primary groups and the state (the extent to which this mediation has meaning for the individuals involved is discussed in the previous section). It is much easier to demonstrate the mediation function of voluntary associations if concrete kinds of organisations are mentioned. Professional associations mediate between their membership and the government especially in such matters as licensing, research funds, and legislation: in these areas, mediation shades off into lobbying. Through their public relations and public information programs, professional associations mediate between their membership and the general public. In national churches, both local and special-interest organisations are voluntary associations that mediate between the individual members and the hierarchy. (Other examples of mediating functions are given in the section "classification into types").

Integration of subgroups: In plural societies, voluntary associations may serve to integrate minority groups into the national society. In fact, many ethnic associations are formed for this express purpose—for instance, the Water Level Society in Japan (as association of the eta that seeks to raise this outcaste group to the level of the national society), or the National Association for the Advancement of Coloured People (NAACP) in the United States. Many ethnic associations are formed for the purpose of maintaining ethnic identity, but as Mary B. Treudley demonstrated in her study of Greek American Associations in Boston, a more frequent result is "the transformation of peasants into citizens" (1949a 1966, p. 59). The success of such organisations can lead to their own disintegration, thus, Kurt Lewin pointed out, with specific reference to American Jewish organisations, that "the task of organizing a group which is economically or otherwise underprivileged in seriously hampered by those members whose real goal is to leave the group rather than promote it" (1948, 1950, p. 193).

Affirmation of values: Voluntary associations may serve as a legitimate locus for the affirmation and expression of values, as do patriotic societies and political parties. Tocqueville recognized the dangers to a society inherent in "the unrestrained liberty of association", but he also recognized the positive aspects of over organisations.

This perilous liberty offers a security against dangers of another kind, in countries where associations are free secret societies are unknown. In America there are factions, but no conspiracies (1835, 1945, Vol. 1, pp. 202-203).

Governing: It was noted above that the uniqueness of the American pattern of voluntary associations has been overstated by many observers: many other countries have large numbers of active associations. What is difficult to overstate, however, is the part played by voluntary associations in the actual business of governing the United States, in the sense of making decisions on policy and of providing services to citizens. Tocqueville was impressed by this: "Wherever at the head of some new undertaking you see the government in France, or a man of rank in England, in the United States you will be sure to find an association" (1835, 1945, Vol. 2, p. 114). Rossi concluded, on the basis of a study of the leadership of a Midwestern industrial city of about 45,000 that he named Mediana, that this pattern is, if anything, more prevalent today than it was at the time of Tocqueville's visit:

The most striking characteristic of contemporary cities, compared with the American community in the nineteenth century, is the relative drop in the importance of local government, not only in its relation to state and federal governments but also in its relation to local voluntary associations. To understand what is happening within a contemporary community an investigator cannot confine himself to the official table of organisation for municipal government but must add to it a host of voluntary associations which act on behalf of the community and which together with the formal structure of local government form the basic organizational framework of the local community. (Rossi 1961, p. 301).

The nature and importance of voluntary association's activity in community decision making probably varies with the size of the community, although to my knowledge there are no data to support this observation. In large cities, voluntary associations seem to serve largely as important pressure groups; in medium sized cities they virtually run the municipal government. Thus, according to Rossi, "There is saying in Mediana to the effect that Rotary owns the town, Kiwanis runs it, and the Jaycees do all the leg work" (1961, p. 309). In small towns the decision-making role is filed by families and cliques, leaving to voluntary associations such service tasks as raising funds for the library, decorating the plaza, and maintaining the cemeteries. Throughout most of America, in fact, almost everywhere except in large cities voluntary associations perform the fundamentally governmental function of coping with emergencies; sickness is treated in voluntary health centres and hospitals;

fires are fought by volunteer fire departments disaster relief is furnished through the American Red Cross. This pattern is, of course, not confined to America: community service organisations are found in many countries. In Florence, for example, although Italy is not known for the importance of its secular voluntary associations, a voluntary association provides the major ambulance service.

The governmental functions performed by voluntary associations at the State and local level are also important. The organisational machinery for the licensing of such professional as lawyers and physicians, for example, is generally run by voluntary professionals societies. Throughout the federal government, agencies rely upon voluntary associations not only for research and training services, and for carrying out public information campaigns but also, in many cases, for the actual administration of the agency's program. Examples are the services provided by the National Travellers Aid Association to the Department of Labour, the services of the Institute of International Education and many other organisations to the foreign student program of the Department of State, and the hundreds of community action agencies that carry out the antipoverty program of the Office of Economic Opportunity. In a review of the financial and policy problems generated by the delegation of governmental functions to voluntary associations, Alan Pifer concluded that "the use of non governmental organisations to carry out public functions, a rare occurrence before World War II, is now accepted policy in most parts of government" (1966, p. 4).

Initiating social change: Since most voluntary associations are formed for the purpose of bringing about some change in society, and since most have had some measure of success in this, it follows that the initiation of social change is one of their major functions for society. The limiting case of social change revolution demonstrates the point; historically, revolutions either have been started by voluntary associations or have been directed by them once mass unrest led to outbursts of violence (see *Revolution*).

In many countries, most of the services that are now assumed to be the responsibility of government were initiated by voluntary associations. This is particularly true to welfare services to the poor, the ill, the orphaned, and the aged, but it is also true of such services as education. In many of the developing countries, for example, the present public school system is modelled after schools established by missionary societies, and these societies often continue to sponsor the secondary schools in which many members of the future elite are trained. This pattern is not confined to non-Western societies: the public school system of New York City, for example, is the successor to a voluntary association the Public School Society.

The prevalence of the pattern in which voluntary associations initiate functions that are subsequently assumed by the government raises the question of whether the widespread utilization of voluntary associations is a permanent feature of Western Society or merely a transitional phase between inactive governments and the welfare state. This question was seriously examined by a number of groups in post-war Britain when the Labour government assumed responsibility for many welfare programs previously carried out by voluntary associations (see for example, Beveridge and Wells 1949). The conclusion reached as a result of these inquiries was that voluntary activities in the welfare field would undoubtedly diminish in importance but would not disappear. In the United States, the assumption of broader welfare responsibilities on the part of the federal (as well as State) government has undoubtedly been beneficial to voluntary health and welfare agencies, since governmental funds are a welcome supplement to gifts made by individuals and private foundations. (See *Planning, Social,* article on *Welfare Planning*).

Distributing Power: The doctrine of political pluralism, which asserts that the power of the sovereign State must be balanced by the power of dispersed associations, is generally said to have had its origin around the turn of the century in the writings of Durkheim, Figgis, Gierke, Maitland, and others. It was Tocqueville, however, who gave classic expression to the notion that the power of the sovereign State is best limited by voluntary associations.

The book Union Democracy (Lipset et al 1956), on one level a case study of a democratically controlled trade union, is on a much broader level, an elaboration of ideas first expressed by Tocqueville in Democracy in America. Here is Lipset's summary of Tacqueville's contribution to an understanding of this aspect of the function of voluntary associations:

His study of America suggested to him two institutions which might combat the new Leviathan (a powerful State ruling an apathetic mass society): local self-government and voluntary associations. Involvement in such institutions seemed to him a basic condition for the stability of the democratic political system. By disseminating ideas and creating consensus among their members, they create the basis for conflict between one organization and another. And, in the process of doing so, they also fulfil certain other roles; they limit the central power, they create new and autonomous centres of power to compete with it, and they help to train potential opposition leaders in politically relevant skills (1959, p. 88).

To test this theory of Tocqueville's would require a vast research program—a program that is well under way in the 1960s through the research of organisational sociologists, political sociologists, and political scientists. There is widespread agreement among these scholars that the two societal trends that have characterized the twentieth century will continue, the extension of social and economic equality and the centralization of power in the hands of government and large organisations. If these trends are not to lead to an Orwellian mass society, new sources of power must be created and maintained. As Tocqueville formulated the problem:

Among the laws that rule human societies there is one which seems to be more precise and clear than all others. If men are to remain civilized or to become so, the art of associating together must grow and improve in the same ratio in which the equality of conditions is increased. (1835), 1945, Vol. 2, p. 118.

By stating the relationship between power and equality in the form of a scientific law. Tocqueville earned the right to be called one of the first truly modern social scientists.

Trade Union

The exact form which trade unions take varies between countries but there is common agreement about the general meaning of term. An early definition is that "A Trade Union is a continuous association of wage earners for the purpose of maintaining or improving the conditions of their working lives. This is an accurate short description if by wage earner is meant all people who sell their labour irrespective of the precise form to their payment takes and if for 'conditions of their working lives' is substituted their standard of living.

The adequacy of such a definition may be tested in the light of four principal criteria:

1. The first criteria is that of a union's personnel. The only stipulation is that they must be free to sell their labour for money. A trade union may consist of members of one trade, occupation profession or industry, a number of these or a combination of them. The members may be wage or salary earners, labourers or higher management. Trade Unions are no longer peculiar to manual workers.
2. A second criterion is that of objectives. These must be primarily industrial but they can and often do, have a political content. This occurs when it can be seen that the primary industrial objectives can only be secured by Government action and/or when the Government plays a dominant role in

economic affairs. Political aims them are normally subsidiary to industrial ones and in the main supplement them. The objectives are continuously widening. At first they were confined to work shop activities. Now they cover a wide range of workers' interests, indeed everything which enters into their standard of living. Trade unions are mainly sectional organisations and their objectives directly concern the interests of their members.

3. The third criterion is that of structure. A Trade Union must have a permanent organisation in that its activities run from one industrial incident to another. This is what is meant by continuous.

   A trade union is sometimes described as a voluntary society, i.e. a society which permits eligible persons to go in or secede as they wish. But it is not necessary that this should be so. Compulsory membership has an historical basis, it can be enforced by trade unionist in workshops, by a trade union in agreement with an employer or by law. In practice a high degree of compulsion in our form of another is exercised to obtained and retain members.

4. The fourth criterion is that of *Environment.* Trade Unions belong only to societies which have a permanent, free, employed class. Unless the employed class is permanent the impulse to combine will not exist and without freedom the facilities to combine will be denied. Variations in industrial and political environments have altered the methods and functions of trade unions.

There is no internationally valid legal definition of a trade union. In some countries trade unions have not been defined by law; in other countries legal emphasis has been placed in different ways on the personnel. The methods or the objects of trade unions. Some trade unionism law include employers. Others are confined to a narrow category of workers, where the law has intervened it has been to restrict the trade union as a social phenomenon, for example by regulating its activities or the conduct of its organisation. Because of this factor the legal definition often varies from common usage.

Voluntary Organisation and Child Labour

Few abuses of human rights are so universally condemned, but at the same time so universally practiced as the child labour. Given the implication of this practice, this issue should rank high on the global agenda. However, in reality it is surrounded by a wall of silence and it is perpetuated by ignorance, child labour continues to be an affront to the conscience of the world community.

Child labour is a reality but there are many myth associated with it in different communities in global perspective. However, when we analyse the grass root situation with emperical data then we are at dismay and disarray. Not understanding the complex cultural situation we are experimenting with the programmes of child labour. The elimination of child labour programme is going to meet the same fate which other such ambitious programmes has met. Before making any conclusion I am giving you a case study of Child Labour Project Society, Nalanda, Bihar where I had been to a faculty member of this Institute to observe and guide the field situation on three different occasions.

Child Labour Project Society, Nalanda, Bihar, India

Introduction: The Child Labour Project Society, Nalanda was established in the year 1995-96 according to the guideline of the Government of India, it was finally registered under Society Registration Act, 1860 in March 1996, with District Magistrate as its Chairman. In addition to the Chairman a number of State Government officials such as DDC, SDO, Dy. S.P., Civil Surgeon, District Welfare Officer, Director DRDA, and District. Labour Superintendent were made members of the society. A few representatives from NGOs and Social Works were included in the society. Assistant Director, Social Security was made its Secretary.

Objectives

The major objective of the society is to rehabilitate unfortunate child labour engaged in various hazardous activities such as Biri making, carpet weaving, rag picking, brickkin and stone chipping, etc.

The specific objectives of the society are as follows:

(a) To lawfully carry out surveys, identification and liberation of child labour/bonded child labour in the district of Nalanda;
(b) To rehabilitate child labour by setting up rehabilitation centre;
(c) To work among other disadvantaged children and working out human and scientific rehabilitation methods for this group;
(d) To work in close co-ordination with the local administration and the State Government in accordance with the guidelines of the Government of India in this regard.

NCLP At Work

In the year 1995-96 the Government of India has sanctioned 25 special schools to the district for the rehabilitation of children engaged in Biri making or other hazardous activities. In the same 4 special school were established in Bihar Sharif Municipality viz. Imadpur, Jhinager, Basar Bigha and Baignabad Mohala in which altogether 400 child labour were enrolled, out of which 209 were boys and the rest were girls. Almost all the children in these schools engaged in Biri making.

Between February 21, and March 3, 1997 a series of public meetings were held at 14 different places in the district. During the public meeting the local people were informed about the objectives of the schools were made through interview from among the local residents. By the end of the April 1997, 14 more schools were made operational. Thus, till now altogether 18 school are functional in the district. Out of the total 25 sanctioned schools to the Nalanda District. The responsibilities of running the schools were assigned to different voluntary organisation having some experience in the area of Child Labour and Education and Rehabilitation.

Out of the total 18 operational special schools in six districts are located in the rural area while the rest twelve are in the urban area of the Biharsharif Municipalities. The total sanctioned strength of one school is 100 children. The total enrolment in 18 schools is 800 children out of which 54.8 per cent are boys and 45.2 per cent are girls. Out of the total enrolled children majority (74.4 per cent) belong to the majority community and 10.3 per cent are from the Scheduled Castes communities.

The appointment of the teachers and other supporting staff in the schools except 4 schools, which were opened during the first phase were made on the basis of interview by the selection committee which was headed of the Project Director and Secretary, NCLP some of the members of the executives also participated in the interview out of the total 54 teachers, 31 are males and the rest are females (23). Among the teachers majority (55.4) belong to the minority communities. Educationally majority (22) of the teachers are Graduate followed by intermediate and matriculates.

Survey

When the Child Labour Project was launched in the district of Nalanda. 21 NGOs were involved in the survey for identification of

Child Labour. During the survey altogether 3730 households were contacted in which 9315 children were found to be between 6—14 years of age. Out of the total children in the age groups of 6—14 years 6083 were reported to be Child Labour engaged in the hazardous work. Out of the total identified child labours 53.04 per cent were boys and the rest were girls.

In view of the directive of the Hon'ble Supreme Court issued on December 10, 1996. A massive survey for the identification of the Child Labour engaged in hazardous activities was taken up in the district between May 12—20, 1996.

During the survey altogether 5996 child labour were identified in the district. Out of which 3035 were boys and 2961 were girls. Out of the total children majority (95.2 per cent) were engaged in Beedi making followed by weaving (2.5 per cent), carpet industries (1.6 per cent), Printing Press (0.3 per cent) and other activities such as leather processing, fire works manufacturing and soap making.

Awareness Generation Programme (AGP)

Before opening of the special school in the district a massive AGP was launched. A number of camps at different localities were held to make the people aware about the evils of the child labour and its consequences.

A month long awareness camp was organised at Rajgir on the occasion of Malmas Mela which has great religious importance in the State of Bihar, the camp was very successful in disseminating informations about the evils of Child Labour among the rural folk who came to Rajgir.

Between February and March at a series of camps were organised during the camps the local residents and the parents of the child labour were made aware about the objectives of the programme and school as well as the facilities available at the schools.

Future Plan

Considering the number of identified child labour engaged in hazardous activities in the district it proposed to open 25 more special schools which will increase the total number of special school to 50 in the district. It has already been mentioned that in the district of Nalanda altogether 5996 child labour were identified during the survey. Thus, it is felt that 25 schools is not sufficient to accommodate such a large number of child labour because the total strength of a school is 100. The location of fresh school would based on the data available through survey. The proposed areas are Islampur, Rajgir, Ben, Silao, Giriyak Rahui and Chandi which needs to be covered under the programme. In some of the blocks the number of schools needs to be increased in order to cover all the identified Child Labour in the District.

Finance

The entire project cost is met by the Ministry of Labour, Government of India. However, it is tell that the funds provided by, the ministry in not sufficient enough to provide adequate nutrition to the children. In the absence of fund for basic infrastructure of the school such as furniture, etc. the organising NGOs have made all the necessary arrangement of their own for better functioning of the special schools.

In the absence of fund for basic infrastructure for the school organising NGOs home made all the necessary arrangement for the proper facility of the school.

School wise Enrolment of Child Labour

Location	*Boys*	*Girls*	*SC*	*Minority*	*Total*
Imadpur	57	43	00	63	100
Jhingnagar	53	47	00	79	100
Basar Bigha	56	44	00	71	100
Baignabad	43	57	00	86	100
Banaulia	56	44	09	91	100
Saluganj	52	48	00	95	100
Mahalpar	51	49	40	09	100
Katarapar	53	47	12	78	100
Kohna Sarai	58	42	03	96	100
Gagandiwan	52	48	00	100	100
Sohdih	56	44	15	40	100
Shekhana	66	34	02	93	100
Bhainsasur	45	55	06	79	100
Burha Nagar (Islampur)	55	45	05	95	100
Haidarganj (Karah)	57	43	10	87	100
Jhalar	58	42	37	33	100
Andhana	51	49	09	63	100
Toofanganj	68	32	37	09	100
Total	987	813	185	1267	1800
Percentage	54.83	45.17	10.3	70.39	100.0

Partner NGOs

1. Jan Jagaran Sanstha Kagjee Mahala

Bihar Sharif

2. Bhartiya Jan Uthan Parisad
Qummruddinganj, Bihar Sharif
3. Nisha Bunai-Silai School
Qummruddinganj, Bihar Sharif
4. Community Unit Slum Area,
Baiganbad, Bihar Sharif
5. Bhartiya Jan Kalyan Seva Samiti
Moughal Kuan, Sohsarai, Nalanda
6. Shama Vikas Samiti
Malah Bigha, Islampur, Nalanda
7. Fellowship of Charities
Sherpur, Bihar Sharif, Nalanda
8. Magadh Jan Uthan Kendra
Oknawa Camp, Qummruddinganj, Bihar Sharif
9. Din Awam Berozgar Sakha
Mathuria (Kamra) Bihar Sharif, Nalanda
10. Samrg Gram Vikas Samiti, Bind Camp
Ramchanderpur, Bihar Sharif, Nalanda
11. Shanti Doot
Garh Par, Bihar Sharif
12. Samaj Seva Kendra
Naland, Silao, Nalanda
13. Gramin Mahila Vikas Sanstha
Sohsarai, Nalanda
14. Rashtra Ratan Samaj Kalyan Sansthan
Sohsarai, Nalanda
15. Janta Karah Kalyan Samaj
Qummruddinganj, Bihar Sharif, Nalanda
16. Uma Gramin Vikas Sanstha, Bharaopar, Bihar Sharif,
Nalanda
17. Magadh Samaj Kalyan Pratisthan, Rajgir, Nalanda
18. Mahila Samaj Vikas Sansthan
Sherpur, Bihar Sharif, Nalanda

Observations

From three visits to field in order to collect emperical data, the observation sheets used during visits following points emerged pertinently:

1. That the child labour elimination programme is celebrated as a festival and ritual by its functionaries and voluntary

organisations because of financial augmentation of the voluntary organisations. Child Labour Elimination Functionaries (CLEF).

2. Most of the CLEF are overburdened with other such programmes of the Government and are frequently engaged in solving the law and order problem of the Government machinery.
3. Most of the CLEF do not have clarity of their role performance.
4. There is a gap between theoretical programmes of the child labour elimination programme and in the realistic situation.
5. Most of the child labour elimination functionaries at the middle and grass root level are not aware of the basic facts about child labour and its enforcement rule which is a part of their day to day activity.
6. No research techniques, methodology is followed in accordance with the rule of the social science.

The Educational Input

7. The nature of education provided to the child labour in the school is quite useless since they are just made literate.
8. Training in vocational courses is a must for the success of the child labour elimination programme, otherwise after spending the period in school they are again working as child labour.
9. The enrolment in the school should be strictly of the child labour only; it has been observed that even those who are not the child labour are getting themselves enrolled to avail the facility of scholarship and tiffin.
10. The scholarship must be paid monthly. It has been observed that it is paid generally after the lapse of six to eight months. Scholarship paid at a time is attracting the attention of the parent of the children which is making parents, and the functionaries corrupt. If it is paid each month then it is not such a sum for which corrupt practices will be adopted.
11. The tiffin must be of indigeneous commodity but generally it is fried rice or two pice of bread or biscuit. Generally fruits like Papaya, Banana, Guava, etc., are locally produced are rich in nutritional value. It has been found that some of the parents of the child labour are growing these fruits, if it is purchased from them and distributed among the children then it will give additional economic inputs to the target group.

Teachers

12. The teachers of these schools should be of missionary zeal. They need to be properly and formally oriented in the child labour elimination programme. In real situation they take it as a job which it is not the recruitment process, the honorarium paid to them per month, their qualification and experience for this job needs to be restructured according to the demand of the programme.

Suggestions

It is said that the programme lack the indigenous approach. In a country like India where we have vast natural resources, we ought to tap and link the indigenous raw materials with such an important programme. Children are the future of the country and future can be turned into reality when world view, ethos, ecology and environment of the target group is taken into account. We have to do heart searching as to how much relevant and successful this programme is.

APPENDIX

Joint Forest Management: Hope on the Horizon

Role of the members of Scheduled Tribes, Scheduled Castes and other weaker sections of the society

Introduction

Manifold depletion of natural resourses in the country in recent decades has been a major source of concern among the planners, social scientists, foresters and intellectuals alike. Human environmental relations are confronted with major problems due to degradation of Forests. Degradation continues unabated with the pressure on land combined with the commercial exploitation of the forests. Local Communities are usually the most immediate and adversely affected by such degradation. Millions of people live inside of in the periphery of forest land depending on its resources for their sustenance. With the degradation of forest the life of these local communities too deteriorates as the socio-economic and cultural systems of these people are inter-linked with the ecology of the forest. Traditional forest management which relied on force, fences and firearms to protect the forests left a lot to be desired and forest management programmes have been re-oriented so as to respond to the local community's needs also. Only when the preservation needs coincides with the interests of the local communities can forests be effectively protected. Thus, the local communities must be motivated to identify themselves with the development and protection of forests by making the forest produce available to them preferentially. The recognition of this point of view in recent times have given rise to the new concept of "Participatory" or "Joint Forest Management" (JFM)

What is JFM?

JFM is a new system of forest management based on the cooperative interaction between Forest Department and local communities to protect forests lands from degradation which is taking place at an alarming rate. In this system of Managements the Forest Department and the local communities become equal partners in protection, regeneration, management and benefit sharing. The strategy is to create employment opportunities for the local communities through resource building activities and sharing of benefits. Resource development activities are identified taking into concideration their needs and priorities and the physical potential of their environment. Micro plans are thus prepared in consultation with community members giving them a variety of options to choose from. In JFM emphasis is given on regeneration of natural forests through protection rather than afforestation as it is monetarily beneficial and more effective. In principle, JFM envisages collection of Non Wood Forest Products (NWFPs) to be more important than production of timber which was the main objective of traditional forest management.

The Kuru Experience

In the late sixties, Wight Village Panchayats were given free hand in management of Forests in Kuru Beat of the erst while Ranchi Forest Division. This was continued for five or six years, then actually the programme could not be implemented due to lack of motivation.

The Arabari Experience

The concept of JFM was first experimented with in 1971-72 in the Arabari reserve range of East Midnapur division in the State of West Bengal. It covered an area of 1272 houses., and consisted of 11 villages with a total population of 168 households. Due to the heavy dependence of the local populace on this range, the Divisional Forest Officer found it necessary to involve the villagers in protection activities. The local people who were conscious of the demerits of deforestation when assured of a source of livelihood during the lean period agreed to render full support. This would enable the forest to regenerate and regain productivity. The entire range of 1272 houses were demarcated and brought under the purview of plantation scheme. The work commenced during the lean period providing the local people equal employment opportunities. A Forest protection committee consisting of twenty two persons from the eleven partaking villages was constituted and under the aegis of this committee various labour generating schemes were implemented. The Committee was also given rights to the collection of all NWFPs. Fuel and fodder needs of the villages were also taken care of. One man and one woman from each village guarded the forest during the day time along with the forests guards. Unauthorised people spotted cutting wood were caught and fined. If a member of the committee was at fault he/she was severely reprimanded by the committee. Given the exclusive rights to restrict access and use of NWFP and a share in the timber, the villages surrounding the Arabari forest tracts effectively protected the forests with the net result of an increase in productivity.

The experience encouraged the West Bengal forest department to formulise the partnership through a special Government order which entitled communities of get 25 per cent of the final yield from the sale of pole timber at the end of the 10-15 year rotation. The success of Arabari prompted not only other parts of West Bengal but also other states to experiment with this new system for rejuvenating degraded forests. Of the 25 states in India, 14 have already issued orders for JFM of their forest areas.

Main Features

In a major shift from the earlier system of forest management the Ministry of Environment and Forests, Government of India issued policy instructions to all State Forest Departments on June 1st 1990, promoting active participation of local communities and NGOs in the regeneration, management, protection of degraded forest tracts. The major provisions of these guidelines are given below.

1. The programme should be implemented under an arrangement among the voluntary agency/NGO, the village community (beneficiary) and the State Forest Department. No ownership or lease right over the forests land should be given to the beneficiary or to the voluntary agency/NGO

2. The beneficiaries should be entitled to a share in usufructs to the extent and subject to the condition prescribed by the state Government. The voluntary agency/NGO should not be entitled to usufructory benefits.

3. Access to forest land and usufructory benefits should be only to beneficiaries who get organised into a village institution, specifically for forest regeneration and protection, the beneficiaries should be given usufruct like grasses, lops and tops of branches and MFPS. If they successfully protect the forest, they may be given a portion of the proceeds from the sale of trees when they mature.

4. Areas to be selected for the programme should be free from claims of any person who is not a beneficiary under the scheme. The selected site should be worked out in accordance with a working scheme (protection,

natural regeneration) duly approved by the State Government. Such scheme may remain in operation for a period of ten years and revised/renewed after that. The working scheme should be prepared in consultation with the beneficiaries.

5. For raising nurseries, preparing land for planting and protecting the tree after planting, the beneficiaries should be paid by the forest department.

6. It should be ensured that there is no grazing at all in the forest land protected by the village community, permission to cut and carry grass free of cost should be given so that stall feeding is promoted. No agriculture should be permitted on the forest land.

7. Along with trees for fuel, fodder and timber the village community may be permitted to plant fruit trees, medicinal plants and trees helping soil and water conservation. Cutting of trees either by village communities or by Forest Department should not be permitted before they mature. In case of energy needs, the village communities should be taken into confidence.

8. The benefit of People's participation should go to the village communities and not to commercial or other interests. The selection of beneficiaries should, therefore be done from only those families which are willing to participate through their personal efforts.

9. The Forest Department should closely supervise the works of the beneficiaries/NGOs. Should they fail or neglect to protect the area from grazing or do not perform the operation prescribed in the working scheme in a satisfactory manner the usufructory benefits should be withdrawn within or without paying compensation to anyone for any work that might have been done prior to it.

Success of JFM

A number of factors attribute to the successful functioning of JFM, but most important among them are the co-operative interaction between the Forest Departments and local communities, and the preparation and implementation of an effective micro plan. India's forest policies date back to over hundred years. Under British rule, the state established monopoly control over forests, reserved large tracts for timber extraction, severely restricted the customary rights of local populations to these resources and encouraged commercially profitable species at the cost of species used by the local communities. There was also large scale clearence and felling for railways, ships, bridges, tea and coffee plantations, irrigation projects and crop cultivation to increase the governments land revenue base and so on. After independence, state monopoly over forests continued with the extension and strengthening of British policies. While forests continued to be exploited for commercial gains the local people's rights to NWFPs were further curtailed and they were considered a main hurdle towards forest conservation.

People's participation was restricted to the forestry programmes and sharing of fringe benefits. The forest communities considered the forest officials as usurpers of their legitimate rights. Thus, misunderstanding and conflicts continued and the rift between the forests officials and the local communities widened.

JFM anticipates a totally different approach from the forest officials as well as the local communities, stress is given for opening new communication channels between the two and establishing mutually beneficial cooperative activities. A part from restricting government policies and adoption of a new benefit sharing formula, mass education and environmental awareness programme should be provided to the local communities.

Micro planning is necessary to ensure people's participation in the management of resources, assessment of the needs of the participating community, to regulate the benefit flow to the participants and to identify and highlight local resources. Micro plans are prepared jointly by the Forest Department and the participating committees. The efficient functioning of these plans is ensured by Divisional Forest Officer and Range Officers.

Supportive policies

JFM programmes implemented in many states have not taken a uniform approach due to social, economic and cultural differences. Consolidating the experiences of the States, a uniform module suitable of different regions must be formulated in order to increase the efficiency for JFM. A two day workshop on sustainable forest management was held at New Delhi in September 1990 to discuss various problems of JFM, in which policy makers, foresters, NGO leaders and social scientists from different parts of the nation participated. The participants, many of whom have been associated with pioneering JFM system over the past decade suggested the following steps needed to be taken in establishing a policy supportive to the emergence of successful JFM programmes.

(1) Issuance of State level resolution encouraging the forest department to work with committees in the management of forest lands,

through formation and empowerment of communities protecting forest lands.

(2) The resolution should provide a framework of JFM agreement, resource sharing rights and protection responsibilities, so that the forest officers and rural participants have clear understanding regarding the form of the management partnership.

(3) For low income rural families to participate in JFM programmes. It is essential that material benefits begin flowing as soon as possible. Harvesting of regenerating grasses and leaves can begin during the first year. Enrichment planting activities should emphasis fast growing species.

(4) Some budget provision may also be necessary to support community forest management groups who are deprived of income during the early phases of forest regeneration. This allocation should support employment which will speed ecological recovery and enhance forest productivity.

(5) Government orders should allow NGO participation in assisting forest departments and committees to establish joint protection and management systems.

(6) Resolutions should require communities participating in the JFM activities to develop methodologies to control grazing through social fencing and stall feeding.

(7) As departments expand JFM systems and activities, extensive staff orientation and training is necessary to develop attitudes and approaches which encourage interaction with community forest management groups.

People's Participation under Joint Forestry Management in Bihar

People's participation in Forestry activities was initially started in 1957 in eight Gram Panchayats of Kuru Block in the east while Ranchi District. This proved to be a nonstarter on account of lack of motivation amongst people as well as lack of proper initiative by the Department. This was not actually fully abondoned, but people of localised areas continued protecting this, but the interest gradually decreased due to no policy at Government level to provide benefit out of such forests protected by them.

With the adoption of policy of people's participation by the Government in 1990, a definite policy and programme has been publicised as a result, about 1700 committees have been formed and all efforts are being made to provide Government support in relation to benefit sharing from such forests protected by people.

The State Government issued notification on JFM in 1990. The state Government resolution on Regeneration of Degraded Forests were issued for the constitution of Village Forest Management and Protection Committees (VFMPC's) vide No. Sa. Va. 54/90-5244 V.P. Date 9.11.1990. The sharing of benefits with the local people and the mechanism was decided by Government of Bihar, Forest and Environment Department letter No. Sa. B. Bhu. Vi. 36/934578 V.P. date 27.8.1993. In pursuance to the above the Forest and Environment Department constituted 1652 village Forest Management and protection committees and covered 28.4 per cent of the protected forests in the state of Bihar as per details below:—

Distribution of Scheduled Caste and Scheduled Tribe Population in India (Statewise) 1991

	SCHEDULE CASTE			SCHEDULE TRIBE	
	Total	*SC Popula-tion*	*% of total population*	*ST Popula-tion*	*% of Popu-lation*
India	8,38,584	1,38,223	16.48	67,758	8.08
Andhra Pradesh	66,508	10.592	15.93	4,200	6.31
Arunachal Pradesh	865	4	0.47	550	63.66
Assam	22,414	1,659	7.40	2,874	12.82
Bihar	86,374	12,572	14.55	6,617	7.66
Goa	1,170	24	2.08	N	0.03
Gujarat	41,310	3.060	7.41	6,162	14,92
Haryana	16,464	3,251	19.75	-	-
Himachal Pradesh	5,171	1,310	25.34	218	4.22
Karnataka	44,977	7,369	16.38	1,916	4.26
Kerala	29,099	2, 887	9.92	312	1.10
Madhya Pradesh	66,181	9,627	14.55	15,399	23.77
Maharashtra	78,937	8,758	11.09	7,318	9.27
Manipur	1,837	37	2.02	632	34.41
Meghalaya	1,775	9	0.51	1,518	85.53
Mizoram	690	1	0.10	654	94.75
Nagaland	1,210	-	-	1,061	87.70
Orissa	31,660	5,129	16.20	7,032	22.21
Punjab	20,282	5,743	28.31	-	-
Rajasthan	44,006	7.608	17.29	5,475	12.44
Sikkim	406	24	5.93	91	22.36
Tamil Nadu	55,859	10,712	19.18	574	1.03
Tripura	2,757	451	16.36	853	30.95
Uttar Pradesh	1,39,112	29,276	21.05	288	0.21
West Bengal	68,078	16,081	23.62	3,809	5.59
UNION TERRITORY/ STATES					
Andman & Nicobar	281	-	-	27	9.54
Chandigarh	642	106	16.51	-	-
Dadar & Nagar Haveli	138	3	1.97	109	78.99
Daman & Diue	102	4	3.83	12	11.54
Delhi	9,421	1,795	19.05	-	-
Lakshdeep	52	-	-	48	93.15
Pondicherry	808	131	16.25	-	-

Source: Census of India, 1991.

PROGRESS OF THE JOINT FOREST MANAGEMENT PROGRAMME UPTO 31.3.1996.

Sl. No.	Name of Division	Total No. of PFs	Total Area of PFs (Ha)	No. of JFMCs Constituted	No.of PFs PFs covered by the JFMCs	Total area (Ha) covered by JFMCs
1	2	3	4	5	6	7
1.	Hazaribagh(W)	837	176,524	267	267	73,786.68
2.	Hazaribagh(E)	747	63,625	186	240	123,735.00
3.	Chatra(S)	408	101,828	16	41	23,976.63
4.	Chatra(N)	507	93,372	13	66	13,914.33
5.	Koderma	1405	73,408	44	72	17,929.79
6.	Giridih	405	143,020	44	168	22,573.95
7.	Dhanbad	157	15,555	33	48	2,404.38
8.	Latehar	415	111,736	71	128	36,862.24
9.	Daltonganj(N)	659	126,661	31	28	14,726.26
10.	Garhwa(N)	357	78,705	95	141	46,852.86
11.	Garhwa(S)	298	123,586	48	76	40,867.00
12.	Gumla	818	118,717	119	161	33,471.73
13.	Ranchi(W)	354	73,744	24	25	12,320.44
14.	Ranchi(E)	683	80,182	72	72	9,466.41
15.	Saranda	16	3,988	9	10	3,504.67
16.	Kolhan	24	11,258	13	11	602.00
17.	Porahat	58	15,816	15	15	5,140.16
18.	Chaibasa(N)	582	61,540	43	86	2,314.83
19.	Chaibasa(S)	156	50,875	34	64	25,342.00
20.	Dhalbum	834	51,863	100	100	9,628.00

21.	Deoghar		31,400	44	129	4,529.54
22.	Dumka	1060	148,136	18	60	3,233.28
23.	Banka	22	42,522	44	52	17,280.00
24.	Monghyr	40	41,077	9	5	5,812.00
25.	Jamui	51	34,760	23	23	5,432.02
26.	Sahebganj	234	5,336	40	102	1,105.30
27.	Shahabad	400	179,762	149	193	102,254.00
28.	Gaya	739	136,146	48	175	60,200.00
	Total	12266	2,195,142	1652	2558	719,265.50

SCHEDULED CASTES POPULATION AND ITS PERCENTAGE TO TOTAL POPULATION IN THE STATE AND DISTRICTS

Name of State/District	*Total Scheduled Castes*			*Percentage of Scheduled Caste*			*RANK*		
	Persons	*Males*	*Females*	*Persons*	*Males*	*Females*	*Persons*	*Males*	*Females*
BIHAR	12571700	6569360	6002340	14.55	14.53	14.58			
1. PATNA	560094	297930	262164	15.48	15.37	15.61	15	15	15
2. NALANDA	387648	204920	182668	19.40	19.47	19.32	6	6	6
3. BHOJPUR	413520	219276	194304	14.26	14.44	14.27	21	18	21
4. ROHTAS	545656	289542	256114	18.81	18.87	18.74	8	7	8
5. AURANGABAD	358274	188123	170151	23.26	23.40	23.12	4	4	4
6. JEHANABAD	216083	113069	103014	18.39	18.47	18.30	9	9	9
7. GAYA	788293	409929	378364	29.58	29.57	29.60	1	1	1
8. NAWADA	331997	171973	160024	24.42	24.49	24.34	3	3	2
9. SARAN	301306	154734	146572	11.71	11.81	11.61	30	30	30
10. SIWAN	241867	120307	121060	11.14	11.22	11.06	31	31	31
11. GOPALGANJ	208382	106333	102049	12.23	12.22	12.18	28	28	28
12. P. CHAMPARAN	335249	177612	157637	14.37	14.29	14.45	20	21	20
13. PU.CHAMPARAN	397714	211196	186518	13.07	13.07	13.07	24	24	24
14. SITAMARHI	289884	154432	135402	12.12	12.16	12.08	29	29	29
15. MUZAFFARPUR	464362	242830	221522	15.72	15.65	15.80	13	13	12
16. VAISHALI	425893	221351	204547	19.35	19.81	19.89	5	5	5
17. BEGUSARAI	263116	137867	125249	14.50	14.42	14.59	18	19	19
18. SAMASTIPUR	489985	251670	238315	18.03	17.54	18.24	10	10	10
19. DARBHANGA	365542	190755	174787	14.46	14.42	14.20	17	17	18
20. MADHUBANI	361687	188273	173414	12.77	12.84	12.69	25	25	26
21. SAHARSHA	383149	199528	183621	15.48	15.23	15.71	16	16	14

22. MADHEPURA	192443	100663	91775	16.34	16.11	16.60	12	12	12
23. PURNIA	234478	121271	113207	12.48	12.28	12.70	26	27	25
24. KATIHAR	160046	82742	77304	8.77	8.65	8.89	33	33	30
25. KHAGARIA	140026	75551	67475	14.49	14.29	14.71	19	20	17
26. MUNGER	503931	264276	239705	16.47	16.26	16.71	11	11	11
27. BHAGALPUR	333453	176797	156656	10.11	10.00	10.18	32	32	32
28. GODDA	72393	37921	34972	8.46	8.46	8.47	34	34	34
29. SAHEBGANJ	70788	36611	34177	5.44	5.45	5.43	38	38	38
30. DUMKA	104094	53577	50517	6.96	7.00	6.91	35	35	35
31. DEOGHAR	115697	60254	55443	12.40	12.34	12.46	27	26	27
32. DHANBAD	415614	227718	187896	15.54	15.54	15.53	14	14	16
33. GIRIDIH	296302	150970	145332	13.31	13.45	13.48	23	23	23
34. HAZARIBAG	537157	276311	260846	18.37	18.77	19.02	7	8	7
35. PALAMU	614560	317616	296944	25.07	25.01	25.14	2	2	2
36. LOHARDAGA	10919	5573	5346	3.78	3.89	3.76	42	42	42
37. GUMLA	61299	31091	30203	5.31	5.65	5.27	39	39	39
38. RANCHI	123337	64292	58947	5.57	5.33	5.55	37	37	37
39. PUR.SINGHBHUM	77494	39838	37356	4.79	4.71	4.87	41	41	41
40. PAS.SINGHBHUM	89496	45482	44014	5.01	5.00	5.01	40	40	40
41. ARARIA	220148	114876	105272	13.66	13.52	13.74	22	22	22
42. KISHANGANJ	65157	33715	31442	6.62	6.62	6.62	36	36	36

SCHEDULED TRIBES POPULATION AND ITS PERCENTAGE TO TOTAL POPULATION IN THE STATE AND DISTRICTS

Name of State/District	Total Scheduled Tribes			Percentage of Scheduled Tribes			Rank		
	Persons	Males	Females	Persons	Males	Females	Persons	Males	Females
BIHAR	6616914	3357563	3259351	7.66	7.43	7.92			
1. PATNA	5370	2916	2454	0.15	0.15	0.15	27	27	27
2. NALANDA	336	188	148	0.02	0.02	0.02	39	40	39
3. BHOJPUR	7282	4096	3186	0.25	0.27	0.23	26	26	26
4. ROHTAS	47076	24973	22103	1.62	1.63	1.62	19	19	19
5. AURANGABAD	504	305	199	0.03	0.04	0.03	35	35	35
6. JEHANABAD	238	148	90	0.02	0.02	0.02	37	36	38
7. GAYA	1468	849	619	0.06	0.06	0.05	31	31	31
8. NAWADA	1246	603	643	0.09	0.09	0.10	29	29	29
9. SARAN	3231	1682	1549	0.13	0.13	0.12	28	28	28
10. SIWAN	12650	6422	6228	0.58	0.60	0.57	24	24	24
11. GOPALGANJ	19167	9749	9418	1.12	1.13	1.12	22	22	22
12. P.CHAMPARAN	31104	16279	14825	1.33	1.31	1.36	20	20	20
13. PU.CHAMPARAN	1278	687	591	0.04	0.04	0.04	33	33	33

14.	SITAMARHI	394	247	147	0.02	0.02	0.01	40	39	40
15.	MUZAFFARPUR	1156	591	565	0.04	0.04	0.04	34	34	34
16.	VAISHALI	1408	716	672	0.07	0.06	0.07	30	30	30
17.	BEGUSARAI	902	516	386	0.05	0.05	0.04	32	32	32
18.	SAMASTIPUR	542	304	238	0.02	0.02	0.02	38	38	37
19.	DARBHANGA	259	144	115	0.01	0.01	0.01	41	41	41
20.	MADHUBANI	597	325	272	0.02	0.02	0.02	36	37	36
21.	SAHARSA	7359	3841	3518	0.30	0.29	0.30	25	25	25
22.	MADHEPURA	8321	4214	4107	0.71	0.67	0.74	23	23	23
23.	PURNIA	82145	42596	39549	4.37	4.31	4.44	15	15	15
24.	KATIHAR	101792	52257	49535	5.58	5.47	5.70	14	14	14
25.	KHAGARIA	35	26	9	0.00	0.00	0.00	42	42	42
26.	MUNGER	70660	36606	34054	2.31	2.25	2.37	18	18	18
27.	BHAGALPUR	110735	57622	53113	3.46	3.37	3.55	17	17	16
28.	GODDA	216047	109314	106733	25.09	24.40	25.84	8	8	8
29.	SAHEBGANJ	507321	257135	250186	38.99	38.28	39.75	6	6	6
30.	DUMKA	621484	314616	306868	41.55	41.13	42.00	5	5	5
31.	DEOGHAR	119085	60945	58140	12.76	12.48	13.07	10	10	10
32.	DHANBAD	225282	116569	108713	8.42	7.96	8.99	13	13	12
33.	GIRIDIH	271924	139560	132364	12.22	12.16	12.28	11	11	11
34.	HAZARIBAG	250586	129321	121265	8.81	8.79	8.84	12	12	13

35.	PALAMU	443266	226486	216780	18.08	17.84	18.35	9	9	9
36.	LOHARDAGA	162964	82045	80919	56.41	55.98	56.85	2	2	2
37.	GUMLA	816988	408004	408984	70.80	70.26	71.35	1	1	1
38.	RANCHI	964422	490510	473912	43.56	42.55	44.65	4	4	4
39.	PUR.SINGHBHUM	466572	236318	230254	28.92	27.92	30.03	7	7	7
40.	PAS.SINGHBHUM	978069	488892	489177	54.70	53.74	55.70	3	3	3
41.	ARARIA	20819	10839	9980	1.29	1.28	1.30	21	21	21
42.	KISHANGANJ	34830	18107	16723	3.54	3.52	3.57	16	16	17

Source : Census of India, 1991.

POPULATION OF SCHEDULED TRIBES (S.T.) & SCHEDULED CASTES (S.C.)

Total Population	-	86374465 (1991 Census)
Scheduled Tribes	-	6616914
Scheduled Caste	-	12571700
Scheduled Tribes	-	6616914
Male	-	3357563
Female	-	3259351
Scheduled Caste	-	12571700
Male	-	6569360
Female	-	6002340

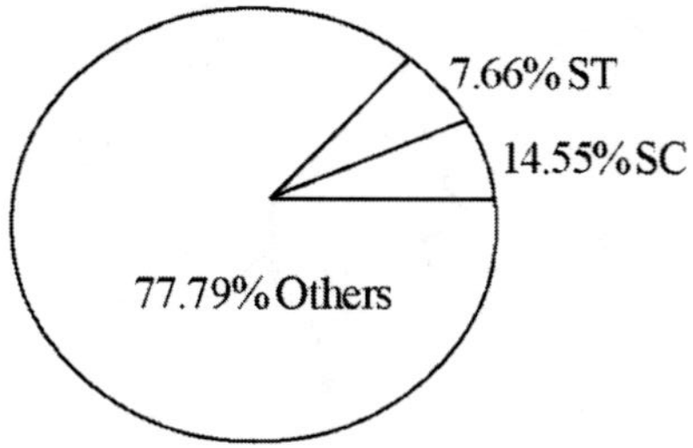

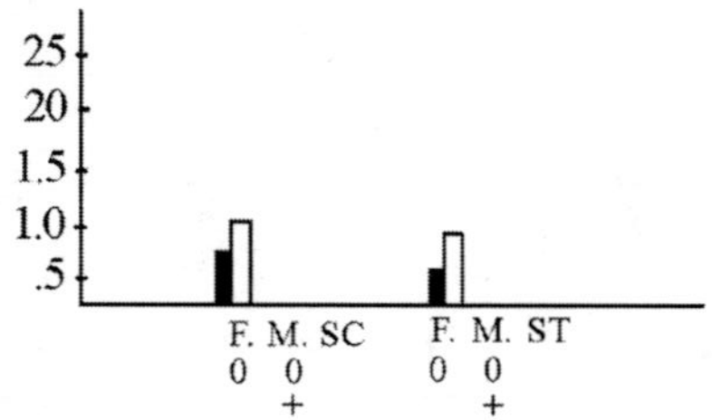

**DISTRIBUTION OF S.T./S.C.
IN THE FOREST OF BIHAR**

Sl.No.	Name of District	Total Pop.	S.C. Pop.	S.T.Pop	S.C%	S.T.%	Rank
1.	W.SINGHBHUM	1787955	89496	978069	5.01	54.70	3
2.	RANCHI	2214048	123239	964422	5.57	43.56	4
3.	GUMLA	1153976	61299	816988	5.31	70.80	1
4.	DUMKA	1495709	104094	621484	6.96	41.55	5
5.	SAHEBGANJ	1301088	70788	507321	5.44	38.99	6
6.	E.SINGHBHUM	1613088	77194	466572	4.79	28.92	7
7.	PALAMU	1649891	423730	317834	25.68	19.26	9
8.	HAZARIBAG	2230931	338489	227099	15.17	10.18	13
9.	GODDA	861182	72893	216047	8.46	25.00	8
10.	DHANBAD	19,49526	312467	171741	16.03	8.31	15
11.	BOKARO	1454416	197365	177123	13.57	12.18	12

12.	LOHARDAGA	288886	10919	162964	3.78	56.41	2
13.	GIRIDIH	1496189	202084	148342	13.51	9.91	14
14.	GARHWA	8,01,350	1,90,830	1,25,432	23.81	15.65	10
15.	DEOGHAR	933113	115697	119085	12.40	12.76	11
16.	KATIHAR	1825380	160046	101792	8.77	5.58	16
17.	PURNIA	1878885	234478	82145	12.48	4.37	18
18.	BHAGALPUR	2010246	196698	59373	9.78	2.95	22
19.	JAMUI	1051527	188666	51490	17.94	4.90	17
20.	BANKA	1192225	136755	51362	11.47	4.31	19
21.	KISHANGANJ	984107	65157	34930	6.62	3.54	21
22.	W.CHAMPARAN	2333666	335249	31104	14.38	1.33	24
23.	BHABHUA	983269	213762	27229	21.74	2.77	23
24.	CHATRA	612713	198668	23487	32.42	3.83	20
25.	ARARIA	1611638	220148	20919	13.66	1.29	25
26.	ROHTAS	1917416	331894	19847	17.31	1.03	27
27.	MUNGER	2008500	315315	19170	15.70	0.95	28
28.	GOPALGANJ	1704310	208382	19167	12.23	1.12	26

29.	SIWAN	2170971	241867	12650	11.14	0.58	30
30.	MADHEPURA	1177706	192443	8321	16.34	0.71	29
31.	BHOJPUR	1792771	266995	5393	14.80	0.30	31
32.	PATNA	3618211	260094	5370	15.48	0.15	36
33.	SUPAUL	1342841	207782	3962	15.47	0.29	33
34.	SAHARSA	1132413	175367	3397	15.49	0.30	32
35.	SARAN	2572980	301306	3231	11.71	0.13	35
36.	BUXAR	1087676	146585	1889	13.48	0.17	34
37.	GAYA	2664803	788293	1468	29.58	0.06	39
38.	VAISHALI	2146065	425898	1408	19.85	0.07	38
39.	E.CHAMPARAN	3043061	397714	1278	13.07	0.04	42
40.	NAWADA	1359694	331997	1246	24.42	0.09	37
41.	MUZAFFARPUR	2953903	464362	1156	15.72	0.04	41
42.	BEGUSARAI	1814773	263116	902	14.50	0.05	40
43.	MADHUBANI	2832024	361687	597	12.77	0.02	47
44.	SAMASTIPUR	2716929	489985	542	18.93	0.02	46
45.	SITAMARHI	2391495	289834	394	12.12	0.02	48
46.	AURANGABAD	1539988	358274	504	23.26	0.03	43
47.	NALANDA	1997995	387648	336	19.40	0.02	44
48.	DARBHANGA	2510959	365542	259	14.56	0.01	49
49.	JEHANABAD	1174900	216083	238	18.39	0.02	45

50.	KHAGARIA	987227	143026	35	14.49	0.0	50
	TOTAL	86374465	12571700	6616914	14.55	7.66	
(A)	CHHOTANAGPUR & S.Ps.	21843911	2589252	6044010	11.85	27.67	
(B)	T.S.T. AREA	10509708	646423	4855216	6.15	46.19	(49.33)
(AA)	CNP & SP Per Cent	25.29	20.60	01.34			
(BB)	TSP Per Cent	12.17	5.14	37.38			
	GROWTH RATE	61-71+21.30	+21.70	+17.31			
	GROWTH RATE	71-81+24.06	+27.57	+17.80			
	GROWTH RATE	81-91+23.54	+23.95	+13.87			

AT A GLANCE FIGURES OF SCHEDULED TRIBES OF BIHAR
POPULATION OF DIFFERENT TRIBES

Sl.No.	*Tribes*	*Population*	*Per Cent of Total Tribal Pop.*	*Literacy*	*Literacy in same tribalcommunity group*
1.	ASUR	7783	0.13	0.08	10.66
2.	BAIGA	3553	0.06	0.02	4.22
3.	BANJARA	412	NEG.	0.02	12.38
4.	BATHUDI	1595	0.03	0.02	16.93
5.	BEDIA	60445	1.04	0.66	10.82
6.	BINJHIA	10009	0.17	0.15	14.52
7.	BIRHOR	4377	0.07	0.03	5.74
8.	BIRJIA	4057	0.07	0.04	10.50
9.	CHERO	52210	0.90	0.92	17.30
10.	CHICH BARAIK	40339	0.69	0.82	20.17
11.	GOND	96574	1.66	1.96	20.00
12.	GORAOT	5206	0.09	0.09	16.61
13.	HO	536524	9.23	9.62	17.71
14.	KARMALI	38652	0.66	0.52	13.30
15.	KHARIA	141771	2.44	3.57	24.86

16.	KHARWAR	222758	3.83	3.89	17.22
17.	KHOND	1263	0.02	0.02	15.99
18.	KISAN	23420	0.40	0.32	13.41
19.	KORA	33951	0.58	0.32	9.28
20.	KORWA	21940	0.38	0.14	6.14
21.	LOHRA	169090	2.91	2.18	12.71
22.	MAHLI	91868	1.59	1.18	12.74
23.	MAL PAHARIYA	79322	1.37	0.61	7.58
24.	MUNDA	845887	14.56	18.98	22.16
25.	ORAON	1048064	18.05	24.71	23.28
26.	PARHAIYA	24012	0.41	0.37	15.30
27.	SANTHAL	2060732	35.47	26.19	12.55
28.	SAURIA PAHARIA	39269	0.68	0.28	6.87
29.	SAVAR	3014	0.05	0.03	9.55
30.	BHUMIJ	136110	2.35	2.26	16.45
31.	UN SPECIFIED	6660	0.1	0.03	3.94
	TOTAL	5810867	100.00	100.00	16.99

Source : Census of India, 1991.

THE DIALECTS OF THE 29 SCHEDULED TRIBES OF BIHAR WITH THEIR LANGUAGE AFFINITIES

SI. No.	Name of Tribe	Dialect	Language Affinities	Remarks
1.	Asur	Asuri	Austro-Asiatic	Russell says that Baiga is a title of priest who are doctors by profession, among the kharwars. Their number was 54 according to 1941 census.
2.	Baiga	Sadani	Indo-Aryan	
3.	Banjara	Sadani	Indo-Aryan	
4.	Bathudi	Mixed	Indo-Aryan	
5.	Bedia	Sadani	Indo-Aryan	A sub-dialect of Bhojpuri
6.	Binjhia	Sadani	Indo-Aryan	A sub-dialect of Bhojpuri
7.	Birhor	A dialect of Mundari	Austro Asianic	
8.	Birjia	Sadani and Bengali	Indo-Aryan	A sub-dialect of Bhojpuri
9.	Bhumij	A dialect of Mundari and Bengali	Austro Asiatic and Indo-Aryan	
10.	Chero	Sadari	..	No language of its own but speak neighbouring Munda language belonging to Austro-Asiatic group
11.	Chik-Baraik	Sadani	Indo-Aryan	A sub-dialect of Bhojpuri
12.	Gond	Gondi	Dravidian	A Dying language superceded by Sadanian Indo-Arayan dialect

13.	Gorait	Sadani	Indo-Aryan	A sub-dialect of Bhojpuri
14.	Ho	Ho	Austro-Asiatic	..
15.	Karmali	Karmali	Austro-Asiatic	Karmali is a subdialect of Santhali
16.	Kharia	Kharia	Austro-Asiatic	A dying language superceded by Sadanian Indo-Aryan dialect
17.	Kharwar	Sadani	Indo-Aryan	A sub-dialect of Bhojpuri
18.	Kisan	..	..	No language of its own but speak neighbouring Munda language belonging to Austro-Asiatic group
19.	Kora	A dialect of Mundari	Austro Asiatic	..
20.	Korwa	Korwa	Austro-Asiatic	Korwa dialect is closely related to Asuri
21.	Lohra	Sadani	Indo-Aaryan	A sub-dialect of Bhojpuri
22.	Mahli	Mahle	Austro-Asiatic	Mahle is a sub-dialect of Santali
23.	Mal-Pahariya	Mahto	Dravidian	..
24.	Munda	Mundari	Austro-Asiatic	..
25.	Oraon	Kurukh	Dravidian	..
26.	Phariya	Sadani	Indo-Aryan	A sub-dialect of Bojpuri
27.	Santal	Santali	Austro-Asiatic	..
28.	Sauria Pahariya	Mahto	Dravidian	..
29.	Savar	Kharia	Austro-Asiatic	The hill kharias are called savars

Note: Almost all the Tribal people speak Sadani with some local variations. Hindi is also intelligible to all with some exceptions.

CLASSIFICATION OF RURAL AND URBAN POPULATION

Total Population	-	86374465	(1991 Census)
Male	-	45,202,091	52.3%
Female	-	41172374	47.7%
Rural Population	-	75021453	
Male	-	39045095	
Female	-	35976358	
Urban Population	-	11353012	
Male	-	6156996	
Female	-	5196016	
Literary Population	-	38.48%	

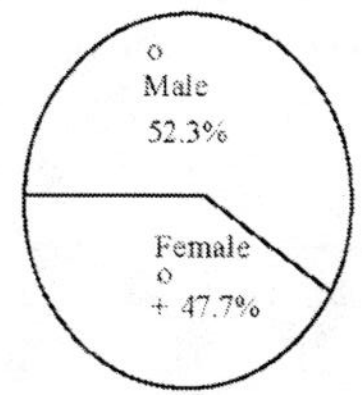

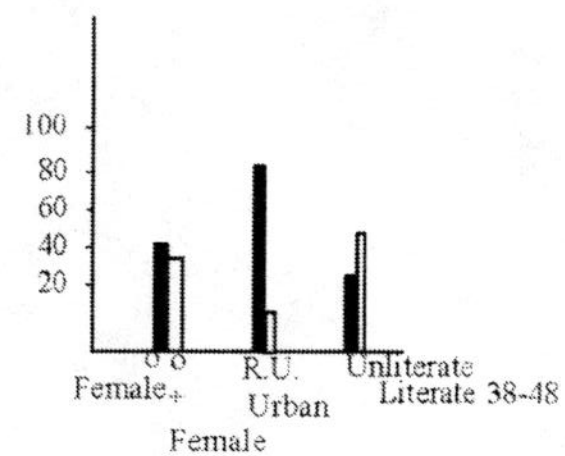

COMPARATIVE DATA REGARDING PUBLIC HEALTH

		Bihar	India
Birth Rate	Rural-	35.1	32.0
Per 1000	Urban-	27.6	25.0
	Combined-	34.4	30.5
Death Rate	Rural-	12.5	11.1
	Urban-	7.9	7.1
	Combined-	12.1	10.2
Infant	Rural-	93	98
Rate	Urban-	63	58
	Combined-	91	91
Leprosy Pervalance Rate		6.9	5
Blindness Incidence		2	1.4
T.B. Pervalance Rate		7.2	5

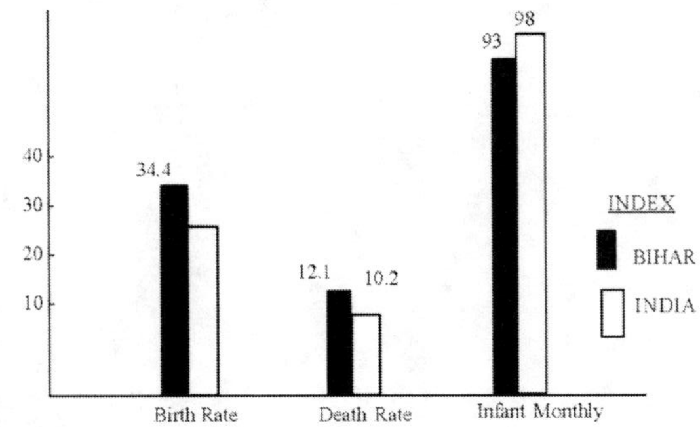

STATEMENT REGARDING RELIGION-WISE FIGURES 1961—81 (BIHAR)

	1961		1971		1981	
	Number	Percentage	Number	Percentage	Number	Percentage
Baudh	3.2	0.7	3.8	0.7	4.7	0.7
Christians	10.7	2.4	14.2	2.6	16.3	2.4
Hindus	368.5	83.5	453.4	82.7	549.7	82.6
Jain	2.00	0.5	2.6	0.5	3.2	0.5
Muslims	46.9	10.7	61.4	11.2	15.6	11.4
Sikh	7.80	1.8	10.4	1.7	13.1	2.00
Others	1.6	0.4	2.2	0.4	2.8	0.4
	438.7	100%	548.0	100%	665.3	100%

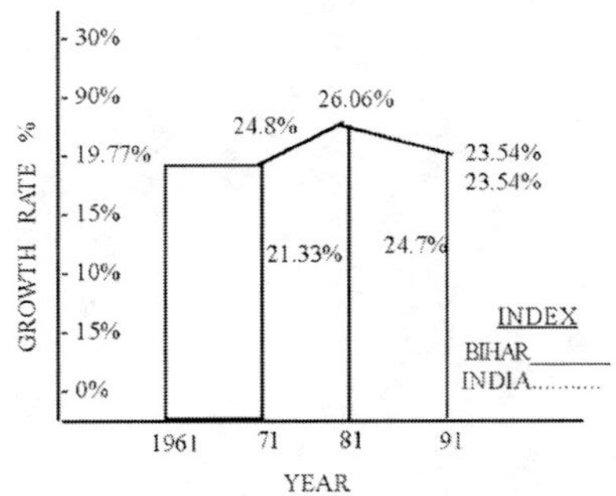

NO. OF OCCUPIED RESIDENTIAL HOUSES (BIHAR)

Year	Houses	No. Village	Density/Km.
1961	6885541 No.	78093	267
1971	8376599 No.	78027	324
1981	9891123 No.	..	402
1991	12833123 No.	77694	497

Shortage of Residential Houses in Per Cent

1951-	9.00%
1961-	15.2%
1971-	14.5%
1981-	21.2%
1991-	29.2%
2001-	39.1%

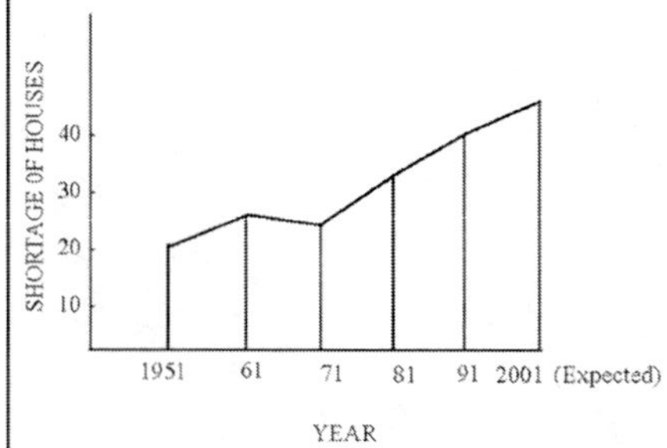

Statement Showing District-wise Land use Pattern in Bihar
(Area in thousands of hectares)

Sl. No.	Year .... District	Total Area of the State by Village paper	Land not available for cultivation: Forest	Barren Land	Land put to Non.Agricultural use	Culturable Land: Total Cols. 4-6	Permanent Pasture & other grazing lands	Culturable Waste other than fallow lands	Land Under misc. tress & groves	Waste Land: Other fallow lands	Current fallow	Total Cols. 18-12	Net area sown	Orchards
	1981-82	17330	2828	1010	1738	5576	138	448	208	961	2060	3815	7860	128
1.	PATNA	317	..	13	52	65	2	3	2	4	26	37	215	2
2.	NALANDA	234	5	1	39	45	..	..	..	..	9	9	179	..
3.	GAYA	651	78	33	65	176	5	7	3	17	116	148	326	1
4.	NAWADA	249	54	11	23	88	2	4	1	3	35	45	116	..
5.	AURANGABAD	330	14	16	41	71	1	13	..	7	79	100	169	..
6.	BHOJPUR	404	..	9	48	57	..	2	1	4	27	31	313	8
7.	ROHTAS	733	180	36	69	285	1	9	1	7	41	59	390	2
8.	SARAN	265	..	18	29	47	..	2	10	4	30	46	171	6
9.	SIWAN	224	..	9	26	35	..	..	5	2	11	18	171	5
10.	GOPALGANJ	204	..	6	21	27	1	2	6	3	16	28	150	4
11.	CHAMPARAN (E).	432	..	8	58	66	1	1	14	5	22	43	322	8

12.	CHAMPARAN (W).	484	92	3	70	165	2	5	10	8	37	62	257	8
13.	MUZAFFARPUR	315	..	6	45	51	1	..	11	5	25	42	221	10
14.	VAISHALI	202	..	24	35	59	..	1	6	2	8	171	126	8
15.	SITAMARHI	265	..	2	45	47	1	..	8	1	13	23	196	6
16.	DARBHANGA	230	..	2	37	39	1	..	7	5	22	35	157	7
17.	SAMASTIPUR	286	..	5	48	53	..	..	12	2	30	44	190	9
18.	MADHUBANI	353	..	2	63	63	1	1	11	3	20	36	253	11
19.	BEGUSARAI	188	..	18	20	38	..	1	2	2	119	24	124	3
20.	MUNGER	784	136	64	81	281	3	22	4	32	113	174	330	3
21.	BHAGALPUR	560	49	66	57	172	5	20	4	21	60	110	279	4
22.	SANTHAL PARGANAS	1422	152	83	113	348	59	83	14	148	238	542	552	1
23.	SAHARSA	583	..	38	90	128	..	..	..	19	71	90	337	7
24.	PURNIA	775	1	29	85	115	4	9	20	20	94	147	513	8
25.	KATIHAR	291	2	22	39	63	1	4	8	8	42	63	164	3
26.	HAZARIBAG	1110	532	89	59	680	15	33	7	89	124	268	162	..
27.	GIRIDIH	688	234	53	45	332	12	30	10	85	95	232	123	..
28.	DHANBAD	299	24	38	68	130	3	20	3	30	47	103	67	..
29.	RANCHI	1822	339	108	99	546	3	74	10	188	214	486	731	4
30.	PALAMU	1273	556	84	43	683	6	24	4	117	221	372	218	..
31.	SINGHBHUM	1357	380	114	125	619	8	78	14	123	155	378	358	..

District-wise Forest Cover (Area in sq. km)

SI. No.	Districts	Geographical Area	Forest Cover 1991 Assesment			Per Cent of forest cover to geographical Area
			Dense	Open	Total	
1.	BHAGALPUR	5589	39	172	211	3.76
2.	PASCHIM CHAMPARAN	5228	482	322	804	15.38
3.	DARBHANGA	2279	..	..	..	..
4.	DHANBAD	2996	7	88	95	3.17
5.	GAYA	6545	292	145	617	9.71
6.	HAZARIBAG	11165	2456	2349	4805	43.04
7.	MUNGER	7908	523	444	967	12.23
8.	MUZAFFARPUR	3172	..	..	..	..
9.	PALAMU	12749	2686	2147	4833	37.91
10.	PATNA	3202	..	..	..	..
11.	PURNIA	7943	5	14	19	0.24
12.	RANCHI	18266	2004	2550	4554	24.93
13.	SAHARSA	5900	..	..	..	..
14.	SANTHALPARAGANA	14206	282	1171	1453	1023
15.	SARAN	2641	..	..	..	..
16.	BEGUSARAI	1918	..	..	..	..

17.	SINGHBHUM	13400	3095	1504	4599	34.22
18.	BHOJPUR	4098	:	:	:	:
19.	GOPALGANJ	2033	:	:	:	:
20.	PURBI CHAMPARAN	1968	:	:	:	:
21.	ROHTAS	7213	585	1043	1628	22.57
22.	SIWAN	2219	:	:	:	:
23.	SITAMARHI	2643	:	:	:	:
24.	VAISHALI	2036	:	:	:	:
25.	MADHUBANI	3501	:	:	:	:
26.	SAMASTIPUR	2904	:	:	:	:
27.	KATIHAR	3057	:	:	:	:
28.	NALANDA	2367	14	14	28	1.18
29.	AURANGABAD	3305	50	77	127	3.84
30.	NAWADA	2494	259	209	468	18.77
31.	GIRIDIH	6892	506	934	1440	20.89
	TOTAL	173877	13285	13383	26668	15.33

Source: The state of Forest Report, 1991, Forest Survey of India, Dehradun.

FOREST RESOURCES IN BIHAR
(Area in thousands of hectare)

District	Land Area	Forest with Density Classification (1) More than 60 %	20.60 %	5.19 %	Bamboo	Scrub	Regroth	Sub total Natural	Plant -ations Forests	Total Forest cover	Forest Cover % of land
AURANGABAD	330.5	0.1	0.2	0.3	0.0	0.5	0.0	1.1	0.0	1.1	0.3
BEGUSARAI	191	0.0	0.0	0.0	0.0	0.2	0.0	0.2	0.0	0.2	0.1
BHAGALPUR	558.9	0.2	2.7	6.0	0.0	2.0	13.8	24.7	0.0	24.7	4.4
BHOJPUR	409.8	0.9	7.0	6.7	0.0	8.6	1.6	24.8	0.4	25.2	6.2
DARBHANGA	227.9	0.0	0.0	0.0	0.0	0.0	0.0	0.0	0.0	0.0	0.0
DHANBAD	299.6	1.0	5.3	2.4	0.0	4.0	6.9	19.5	0.4	19.9	6.7
GAYA	654.5	3.0	8.3	22.6	0.0	15.8	3.1	52.7	3.1	55.8	8.5
GIRIDIH	689.2	15.9	26.9	23.7	0.0	8.0	85.3	159.9	0.4	160.3	23.3
GOPALGANJ	203	0.0	0.0	0.0	0.0	0.0	0.0	0.0	0.0	0.0	0.0
HAZARIBAG	1116.5	45.8	103.4	138.2	0.2	85.8	146.1	519.7	1.7	521.4	46.7
KATIHAR	305.7	0.0	0.0	0.0	0.0	0.0	0.0	0.0	0.0	0.0	0.0
MADHUBANI	350.1	0.0	0.0	0.0	0.0	0.0	0.0	0.0	0.0	0.0	0.0
MUNGER	790.8	34.4	25.0	17.8	0.0	2.2	19.7	99.0	1.0	100.1	12.7
MUZAFFARPUR	317.2	0.0	0.0	0.0	0.0	0.0	0.0	0.0	0.0	0.0	0.0

NALANDA	236.7	0.0	0.0	0.0	0.0	0.0	0.0	0.0	0.0	0.0	0.0
NAWADA	249.4	7.8	16.4	9.9	0.0	4.8	11.2	50.1	0.8	50.9	20.4
PALAMU	1274.9	94.1	130.4	125.8	0.5	86.4	41.1	478.4	1.1	479.5	37.6
PA. CHAMPARAN	522.8	27.0	20.3	5.0	0.0	0.1	0.0	52.3	2.0	54.4	10.4
PATNA	320.2	0.0	0.0	0.0	0.0	0.0	0.0	0.0	0.0	0.0	0.0
PU. CHAMPARAN	396.8	0.0	0.0	0.0	0.0	0.0	0.0	0.0	0.0	0.0	0.0
PURNIA	794.3	0.0	0.0	0.0	0.0	0.0	0.0	0.0	0.0	0.0	0.0
RANCHI	1826.6	105.0	127.5	80.5	0.0	7.6	95.7	416.3	0.3	410.6	22.8
ROHTAS	721.3	8.2	30.6	46.6	0.0	36.0	13.5	134.9	0.4	135.2	18.8
SAHARSA	590.0	0.0	0.0	0.0	0.0	0.0	0.0	0.0	0.0	0.0	0.0
SAMASTIPUR	290.4	0.0	0.0	0.0	0.0	0.0	0.0	0.0	0.0	0.0	0.0
SANTHALPARGANA	1420.6	4.0	5.2	11.9	5.3	6.1	67.4	99.9	0.8	100.6	7.1
SARAN	264.1	0.0	0.0	0.0	0.0	0.0	0.0	0.0	0.0	0.0	0.0
SINGHBHUM	1344.0	229.6	89.9	49.7	0.0	18.4	69.3	456.8	3.2	460.0	34.2
SITAMARHI	264.3	0.0	0.0	0.0	0.0	0.0	0.0	0.0	0.0	0.0	0.0
SIWAN	221.9	0.0	0.0	0.0	0.0	0.0	0.0	0.0	0.0	0.0	0.0
VAISHALI	203.6	0.00	0.0	0.0	0.0	0.0	0.0	0.0	0.0	0.0	0.0
TOTAL	17387.7	577.1	599.0	547.1	6.2	286.2	574.7	2590.3	15.7	2605.9	15.0

Division-wise Status of VFMPCs

Sl. No.	Name of Division	No.of PF	Area of PF (Ha.)	No. of VFMPC	No. of PF being protected by VFMPC	Area being protected by VFMPC (Ha.)
1.	HAZARIBAG (WEST)	837	169137.0	267	267	73786.7
2.	HAZARIBAG (EAST)	747	120950.0	186	240	36862.4
3.	CHATRA SOUTH	408	101892.0	16	41	23976.6
4.	CHATRA NORTH	507	93497.0	13	66	13914.3
5.	KODARMA	17	15838.0	44	72	17929.8
6.	GIRIDIH	1405	138953.4	44	29	22576.2
7.	DHANBAD	157	10928.7	33	48	2404.4
8.	LATEHAR	415	108977.0	71	128	36862.3
9.	DALTONGANJ NORTH	659	128965.0	31	48	14726.0
10.	GARHWA NORTH	357	78568.0	95	141	46852.9
11.	GARHWA SOUTH	298	123940.0	48	76	40867.0
12.	GUMLA	807	118431.0	119	161	33471.8
13.	RANCHI WEST	354	115132.0	24	25	12320.5
14.	RANCHI EAST	683	64257.0	72	72	9466.4
15.	SARANDA	16	3989.0	9	10	3504.6

16.	KOLHAN	24	10486.0	13	11	602.0
17.	PORAHAT	58	15632.0	15	15	4185.0
18.	CHAIBASA NORTH	582	58675.0	43	86	2314.8
19.	CHAIBASA SOUTH	156	53761.0	34	64	25342.0
20.	DHALBHUM	834	40608.0	100	100	9628.00
21.	DEOGHAR	..	..	44	129	4529.6
22.	DUMKA	1060	42215.0	18	60	3233.3
23.	BANKA	122	39062.0	44	52	17280.0
24.	MONGHYR	89	4244.0	9	5	5812.0
25.	JAMUI AFFORESTATION	51	35812.0	23	23	5432.0
26.	SAHEBGANJ	234	5336.0	40	102	1105.3
27.	SHAHABAD	400	178563.0	149	193	102254.0
28.	GAYA	739	149571.0	48	175	60200.0
	TOTAL					6314.399

List of Some Important NTFP Commonly Available in Bihar Forests

A. Fruits and Seeds

1. Sal
2. Mahua
3. Harra
4. Bahera
5. Kusum
6. Aonla
7. Rohini
8. Karanj
9. Piar
10. Kend
11. Bael
12. Tamaarind
13. Bhelwa
14. Karonda
15. Semul
16. Ber
17. Jamun

B. Flowers

1. Mahua
2. Palas
3. Harsingar

C. Bark

1. Medha Chal
2. Pojo Chal
3. Baglar Chal
4. Arjun Chal

D. Leaves

1. Sal
2. Mahulan
3. Khajur
4. Kendu
5. Palas
6. Sisal

E. Gums

1. Sal resin
2. Khair Gum
3. Babul Gum
4. Salai Gum
5. Piar Gum
6. Karaya Gum

F. Grasses

1. Khus
2. Sabai
3. Churrath

G. Medicinal

1. Dudh Koreya
2. Chiraita
3. Dhataki
4. Putri
5. Galphuli
6. Sindaur
7. Antamul
8. Aswagandha
9. Sarpgandha
10. Dudhi
11. Anantmul
12. Amaltas
13. Sataawar

Index